1 English Connects

W0316422

1 ▶ English in Germany

a *Underline the English words in the texts below.*

b *Can you think of (or maybe invent) German words and expressions to replace the English words?*

Besuchen Sie unsere Filiale in der City: Topkonditionen für Leasing, freundlicher Service, große Auswahl.

Innenstadt

Vermietung

Kundendienst

Schon mal was von Total-Body-Make-up gehört? Das ist first class styling von Kopf bis Fuß! Machen Sie mit beim Wellness-Weekend.

Ganzkörperverschönerung

erstklassig

Gestaltung

Wohlbefindenswochenende

Ein Movie über Musik. Ein Girl auf dem Weg zum Star. Während sie jobbt, lernt sie ihre große Liebe kennen. Der Soundtrack erscheint am 16.7.

Film Mädchen

berühmte Persönlichkeit

leistet Gelegenheitsarbeit

Tonspur/Musik zum Film

Outfit für Business-Travellers aus dem BahnShop im eleganten Look.

Kleidung

Geschäftsreisende

Laden

Moderichtung/Aussehen

„Komm, wir machen einen Deal: Ich checke deine Hausaufgaben und du kommst zum Meeting mit unserem Coach."

Geschäft

prüfe

Zusammenkunft/Treffen

Sportlehrer/in; Trainer/in

August: Zeit für Fun, Relaxen und Holidays. Jetten Sie nonstop nach New York. Oder wie wäre es mit Shopping in London?

Spaß

Erholung

Urlaub

Fliegen

ohne Pause

Einkaufen

▶▶▶ Now you

Why do you think people use so many English words in German? Some people think that too much English is used in German. What do you think?

HA

Birligt

2 ▶ Crosswords

√ **a** *Complete the crossword.*

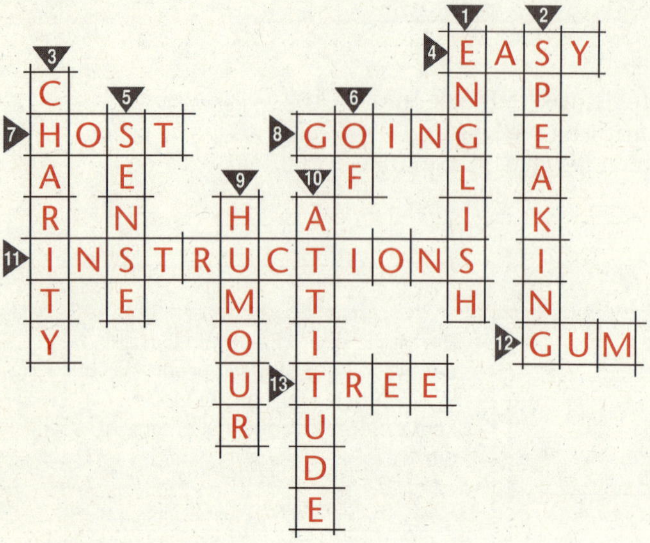

Across ➡

4 & 8 This word describes someone who doesn't take life too seriously.

7 It's someone who welcomes other people into his/her home.

11 It's a piece of writing that you read to find out how to do something, e.g. how to wash clothes.

12 & 13 It's a kind of tree that is found in Australia.

Down ⬇

1 & 2 This word describes a country whose population speaks English.

3 It's an organization whose aim is to collect money for others.

5, 6 & 9 It's the reason that people have for finding some things funny.

10 It's the way that you have of looking at life.

b *Look again at the clues in* **a**. *Underline the* relative pronouns *that you can leave out.*

tip Remember: If there's something between the relative pronoun and the verb, you can leave it out!

√ **c** *Make clues for this crossword and use relative clauses. Leave the relative pronoun out if you can.*

1 *It's something that is* worn by students in British/ Australian schools.

2 It's a person who visits a family or a hotel.

3 It's the number of people who live in a country or an area.

4 It's a text that is written by a reporter for a newspaper.

5 It's a word that describes someone who isn't nervous or shy.

6 It's the animal that is the symbol of Australia.

7 It's a card that shows if you are in school or work.

8 It's a person who buys goods or services.

p. 9/3

3 ▶ BLUE BOX Things you used to do → blue box, p. 141

Think about the things you used to do when you were in Form 3. Write a paragraph about yourself then and how you've changed. Use 'used to' and 'would' as much as you can.

- What did you look like then?
- Did you like school?
- Who did you use to spend time with?
- What did you use to do together?
- Do you still have the same friends/do the same things?

When I was in Form 3 I was very small. I used to like school then because we didn't get so much homework! I used to spend my time with my best friends, Jan and Philip. Jan is still my friend today, but Philip moved away and I don't see him any more. We used to play football all the time, and we collected stickers. Now we collect computer games instead.

p. 9/3

4 ▶ Did you know?

Complete these sentences. Put the extra information from the boxes into non-defining relative clauses.

Indian English is the English spoken in India.

The fact that Shakespeare sounded like an American might surprise a lot of British people.

The Queen and politicians now use the word 'walk-about'.

'Strine' was first spoken by convicts and poor immigrants in Australia.

Cockney is the dialect spoken in the East End of London.

We now think of 'fall' as an American English word.

A British person would say 'leave your name', not 'leave your good name'.

1 Experts think Shakespeare spoke English more like a modern American than a modern Brit, *which might surprise a lot of British people*.

2 'Fall', *which we now think of as an American English word,* was often used instead of 'autumn' in 17th century England.

3 Cockney, *which is spoken in the East End of London,* and 'Strine', *which was first spoken by convicts and poor immigrants in Australia,* are quite similar.

4 Some Australian English words have entered British English. One example is 'walk-about', *which is now used by the Queen and politicians*.

5 Indian English, *which is the English spoken in India,* sometimes sounds a little old-fashioned to speakers of British English.

6 For example, in an Indian office you might be asked to 'leave your good name' rather than 'leave your name', *which a British person would say*.

p. 11/3

5 ▶ In a host family

Tom is a British student staying with you. He hasn't studied German, and your father doesn't speak English. Complete the conversation. If you don't know a word, don't look it up, but paraphrase.

DAD Frag Tom, ob er eine Banane oder Quark mit Trauben haben möchte.

TOM I understood banana, but what's the other dessert?

YOU *It's produced from milk and it's got grapes in it.*

TOM Sounds good. I'd love some. Could you ask if I could have a shower later?

YOU *Er möchte später duschen.*

DAD Selbstverständlich. Wenn er frische Handtücher braucht, die gibt es reichlich im Schrank im Badezimmer. Er soll sich bedienen.

YOU *Of course you can. And you know the things you use to dry yourself? Well, there are loads of them in the cupboard in the bathroom. Help yourself.*

DAD Braucht er einen Fön?

YOU *He asks if you need one of those gadgets for drying your hair.*

TOM Actually I've brought one with me.

YOU *Er hat seinen eigenen mitgebracht.*

DAD Aber wahrscheinlich wird er einen Adapter brauchen, oder?

YOU *Can you use it with the English plug or do you need an extra plug?*

TOM Oh, I don't know. I hadn't thought of that. I'll check. Thanks.

YOU *Er wird nachschauen/-prüfen.*

p. 12/1

6 ▶ ... rewrite these notices

a *Look at the notice below. If you look at the dictionary entry, you'll understand why it sounds strange.*

In a Bucharest hotel:
The lift is being fixed for the next day. During that time we regret that you will be unbearable.

unbearable /ʌn'beərəbl/ *Adj* (*Adv* **unbearably**) /ʌn'beərəbli/ unerträglich

b *Rewrite the notice by completing these sentences.*

Sorry! The lift *isn't working*.

We hope it will be *fixed tomorrow*.

c *Think about the underlined words and work out what is strange about these notices, using a dictionary if you need to. Then rewrite the notices.*

In an Athens hotel:
Visitors are expected to complain at the office between 9 and 11 am daily.

If you have a problem, go to the office any day between 9 and 11 am.

In a Paris hotel:
Please leave your values at the front door.

Please leave your valuables at (the) reception.

p. 13/3

Working with the text

7 ▶ Attitudes

The diagram below shows who talks to who in the first extract of the story on pages 15/16. Choose short sentences or phrases from the story that in your opinion best show the attitudes of the characters towards each other. Write the sentences you choose beside the arrows on the diagram.

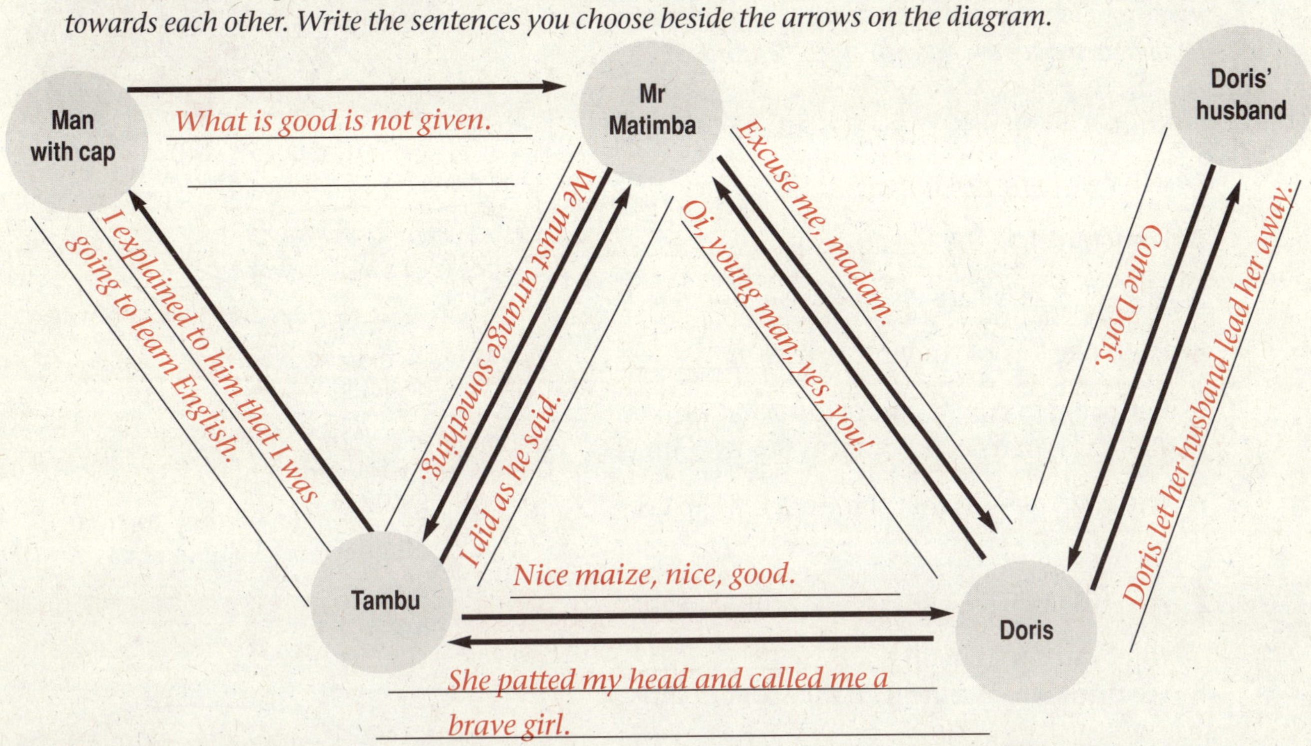

8 ▶ Reading between the lines

What can you tell from the following sentences about what the characters are thinking or feeling at that moment?

1 Doris changed colour like a chameleon. (p. 16, l. 20)

She felt angry that Tambu wasn't at school. When Mr Matimba explained, she felt embarrassed.

2 'What is good is not given.' (p. 16, l. 26)

You can't expect help from people. You have to work for your money.

3 The money, the money – no thought for the method. (p. 16, ll. 4–15)

The most important thing was having the money. It didn't matter that Matimba told lies to Doris.

9 ▶ Would you like to read more?

You've read the two extracts from this book. Would you like to read the rest of it? Why?/Why not?

p. 17

10 ▶ ... find these words

This is a list of important points a teacher wants to make in a letter about an exchange she is planning. Complete the sentences with suitable words.

1 Students will visit three schools and the visits will be simultaneous.
2 French will be the lingua franca.
3 The schools we are visiting are all mixed.
4 We'd like lots of students to take part.
5 I'm going to post more information about our partner schools on our website.
6 The good news is that the students can go for free.
7 This is thanks to a gift from a kind person, who wants to remain anonymous.
8 We think this is a great chance for our girls to make contact with young people from different countries.

11 ▶ ... get it right

Complete the article. Use gerunds *or* to-infinitives *and the verbs from the box.*

be (3 ×) • do • feel (2 ×) • go (2 ×) • have • live • phone • say (2 ×) • see • speak (2 ×) • tell • write

EXCHANGES: A GOOD IDEA – YES OR NO?

I've just come back from an exchange in France and some people have asked me to write an article about being an exchange student. They told me to tell the truth and wanted to know what I had found difficult about living in a foreign country. I think they expected me to be negative about the experience. Well, I don't know what to say. The truth is I loved being there. Of course at the beginning I used to feel a bit homesick and I missed seeing my mates. I remember having one bad day when a friend from home had promised to phone and she forgot to do it until the next day. I remember feeling as if they had all forgotten me! Speaking a foreign language all the time isn't easy. At first I refused to say anything! But now I don't mind speaking French. I definitely recommend going on an exchange. I'm looking forward to going again.

12 ▶ ... do a project in English

How do you say these things in English?

1 Als Hausaufgabe müssen wir Forschungen über die Medien anstellen.
We've got to do research on the media for homework.

2 Wie kommst du mit deinem Projekt voran?
How are you getting on with your project?

3 Es ist so ein schwieriges Thema. *It's such a difficult topic.*

4 Wir haben nichts als Ärger mit diesem Rechner gehabt.
We've had nothing but trouble with this computer.

5 Unterteile die Infos mithilfe von Untertiteln .
Divide the information up with sub-headings.

6 Weißt du, was dieses Symbol darstellt?
Do you know what this symbol represents?

7 Was die Lehrerin sagte, ergab nicht viel Sinn.
What the teacher said didn't make much sense.

8 Ich muss diese Notizen nochmal schreiben. Ich kann sie nicht lesen. *I've got to rewrite these notes. I can't read them.*

13 ▶ ... write about your opinion

Imagine the teachers and parents of your school have had a brilliant idea. They want all students to wear uniform! In 100 words or less, explain why you think this is a good or bad idea.

Useful phrases:
- One good reason for/against this idea ...
- I also think ...
- In my opinion ...
- Another reason ...
- Finally, I would like to say again that ...

I'm writing about the suggestion that students should wear uniform. *I know that uniform is popular in some countries, but I really don't understand why. One good reason against this idea is that uniforms would be very expensive. I also think that it would be very boring if everybody wore the same clothes. Another reason I'm against it is that it would make school very formal. Would our teachers come to school in suits and ties? Finally, I would like to say that in my opinion the teachers and parents should think again on this.*

2 The Best Years of Our Lives?

1 ▶ Facts about you

Read about Billie. Then fill in the facts form for yourself. You haven't got much space, so think hard about your answers before you write.

Real name: Billie Paul Piper
Goal[1]: To be good at what I do.
Do you worry about the way you look?: I think I'm like most girls my age – sometimes I worry about my weight or my hair. But if you start worrying a lot it becomes a real problem.
Is the life of a popstar what you thought it might be? Nobody can imagine how much work it is, but I really enjoy it.
What would you tell your fans? Enjoy your youth while you're young.
How does it feel to be a hero? I've had lots of letters from my fans

Nickname?

____

Do you worry about the way you look?

No, I don't. I'd like long legs. But I can't change that. I think I look OK.

Would you like to be a popstar? Why?/Why not?

I would love the money, but I'd hate the attention of the media.

What's your goal in life?

To make a lot of money. To have a successful career. To buy a house in Mallorca.

Who is your role model and why?

Ronan Keating because he is a very nice person and he thinks about his fans.

What advice would you give to younger kids?

Work hard, but also have free-time activities. It's important to relax.

[1] goal *Ziel*

p. 19/2

2 ▶ Between friends

When you chat, you often repeat what the other person says. But you try to use different words. Complete the sentences below. Don't repeat any of the **words in bold**.

1 You look **worried about something**.
– Yes, I've got something on *my mind* .
2 She always **shouts at me** and **tells me what to do**.
– Don't let her *bully* you!
3 I really **hate** it. – Well, if you *dislike* it that much, don't do it.
4 We can **go to a film, or go bowling**. – Isn't there some other *entertainment* ?
5 I think €50 is a **lot** of money for a jacket. – Yes, it's a huge *amount* of money.
6 She says we **shouldn't talk about it**. – That's interesting, she wants to keep it *private* .
7 Oh, come on. **Nearly everybody** else agrees.
– OK, if the *majority* agrees, I suppose I'll have to agree too.

p. 19/2

3 ▶ What makes a good magazine?

Complete the crossword.

Across

5 Some people change the pictures on their bedroom wall all the time. So they like to find a free … in the magazine.
8 Everybody loves to read about other people's problems. So you have to have an …
9 The first thing people see when they look at a magazine is the … That's why it must be as attractive as possible.
10 Lots of people are interested in clothes. So they want … pages.

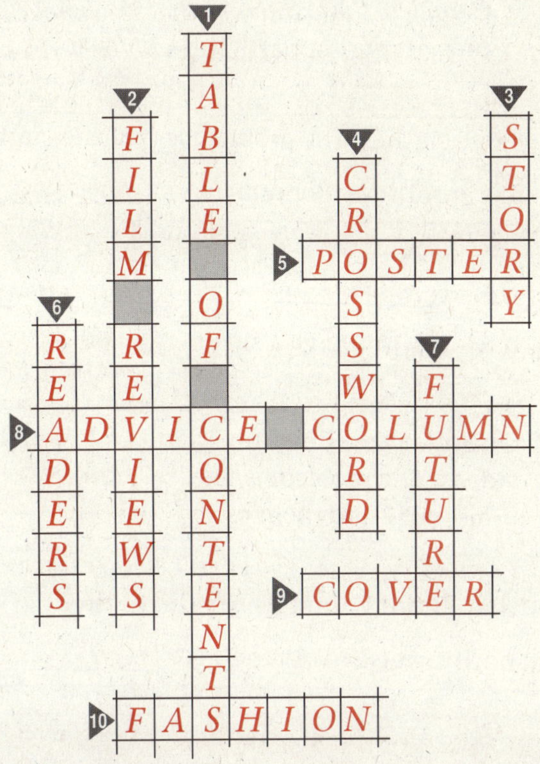

Down

1 People have to be able to find the articles. So you need a …
2 Lots of people want to know about new films. They want to read some good …
3 Some people like to read. So a short … (if possible by a famous writer) will keep them happy.
4 For people who like playing with words or doing puzzles, a … is a good idea.
6 Mags often ask their … to write about their embarrassing moments or their real life stories and they always get lots of letters.
7 The stars page is always popular. Everybody likes to read what the stars say about the …, even if they don't believe it!

▶▶▶ Now you

a *Imagine you have to design a magazine for students in your year at school. Think about these questions and make some notes:*
What would you put on the cover?
What kind of articles would/wouldn't you put in and why?
How could you make it really interesting?

MY IDEAS FOR A MAGAZINE
First of all I'd put a photo of some people in the year on the cover. People always like to see pictures of themselves! Perhaps someone could write a report on the class trip. A lot of funny things happened! Most people would be interested in that. I don't think people would be interested in reading

b *Write about your ideas.*

p. 20/1

4 ▶ Problems, problems

Complete the extracts so that they make sense. Use present *or* past participles *of the verbs in the box.*

annoy • bore • depress • embarrass
frighten • frustrate • understand

I love clothes. The problem is that the clothes that I like are always too small. It's so *depressing* ____.

Don't be *depressed* ____. Just pick a bigger size. Then the clothes will fit you!

My sister is so *annoying* ____! I often wish I didn't have a sister.

I know exactly how you feel. I used to get so *annoyed/frustrated* ____ with my sister. But now she's my best friend. It can happen!

On Sunday evenings my friend and I watch videos. The problem is, he likes horror films, but I find them really *frightening* ____. I can't sleep after that. But if I don't watch them, there's nothing else to do and I get *bored* ____.

I know what you mean. Sunday evenings can be so *boring* ____. And I have a problem with horror films, too. Usually I get really *frightened* ____ and have to hide behind the sofa.

I go red all the time. Even when I'm not *embarrassed* ____, I still go red.

I know it's *embarrassing* ____ but try not to worry too much. Some people might laugh, but most people are more *understanding* ____ than you think.

p. 21/5

5 ▶ Wanted: a hard-working, quick-thinking student

a *Complete the phrases.*

1 a picture that looks crazy → a *crazy* ____-looking picture
2 a boy who speaks German → a *German-speaking* ____ boy
3 a car that moves slowly → a *slow-moving* ____ car.
4 You wrote this letter well. → It's a well-*written* ____ letter.
5 You planned the picnic well. → It was a *well-planned* ____ picnic.

b *Complete the advert.*

Boy, 15, tall, blond, attractive, serious-*looking* ____, hard-*working* ____, quick-*thinking* ____, likes well-*written* ____ science fiction stories, wants to meet trendy-*looking* ____, English-*speaking* ____ girl. Must like football and fast-*moving* ____ cars.

c *Write an advert for yourself. First describe yourself. Then say what kind of partner you are looking for.*

Girl, 16, lively, intelligent, likes old films and well-planned picnics, wants to meet good-looking boy. Must like fashion and be trendy-looking.

____

p. 21/5

Working with the text

6 ▶ Describing a character

a *Look again at the story on pages 22–24. Make notes on Reuben Beardsley in the chart below.*

General	Nickname, reason: Stiff because of way he moved Age, situation: teenage, new Hobbies: none? Eye colour, hair: not said	What do they think of him? They are 'better' than him. How do they behave towards him? criticize appearance and behaviour, invent 'fleas', dirty mag, avoid him Positive things about him: hard-working (?), enjoys talking / teachers (?!)	Relationship to others
What he looks like	Size: 4'7" Clothes: bad!, sensible coat Other information: glasses, thin, 'Mr Spock' ears, spots, Elephant Man	Negative things about him: appearance, bum-licker How he reacts to problems: first nothing (except map). Then: all gets too much, he cries, goes away	What he is like

b *Write about Reuben in your exercise book. Your notes will help you to structure your text.*

7 ▶ What really happened in front of the school?

a *What did this witness see? Complete the report. Write sentences with* present participles *or* infinitives.

1 Two girls were hanging around in front of the school.
He saw two girls hanging around in front of the school.

2 They were shouting at some small kids.
He heard them shout/ing at some small kids.

3 One boy took something out of his pocket.
He noticed one kid take/taking something out of his pocket.

4 One girl hit the boy with her bag.
Then he saw the other girl hitting the boy with her bag.

b *This witness saw something different. Write sentences in the same way.*

1 A gang of small kids was walking through the school gates.
She noticed a gang of kids walking through the school gates.

2 A boy threw stones at two older girls.
She saw one boy throw stones at two older girls.

3 A boy was holding a dead bird in his hand.
She saw a boy holding a dead bird in his hand.

p. 27/7

8 ▶ Crime and punishment

Which verbs from the box can go with the nouns in the table?
Can you think of other nouns that can go with these verbs?

break • catch • commit
damage • hurt • rob • steal

commit	a crime
damage	a car, a phone box, *a building, a bike*
hurt	a child, your arm, *a police officer*
rob	an old lady, a bank, *a house*
steal	a handbag, money, *a camera, a car*
catch	a shoplifter, a criminal, *a vandal, a thief*
break	the law, a criminal, *a rule*

p. 27/8

9 ▶ Reports in the local paper

Imagine an English girl, Jenny, is staying with your family. She has seen these reports in the paper, but she doesn't quite understand them. Give her an idea about what's in them. (Tip: Don't translate everything. Just give the important information.)

Dreiste Ladendiebe
In einem Kaufhaus am Markt fielen zwei Männer und eine Frau auf, als sie wertvolle Pullover stahlen. Das Trio griff den Kaufhausdetektiv an und lief davon. Sie wurden in der Kirchgasse geschnappt.

Autos beschädigt
Im Bereich der Diskothek "Fliegenfalle" wurden gestern Abend mindestens 15 PKW von Vandalen zerkratzt. Eine verdächtige Person wurde verhaftet. Hinweise bitte an die Polizei, Tel. 888-01.

Motorradfahrer übersehen
Ein 42-jähriger Autofahrer übersah beim Linksabbiegen auf der Bahnhofstraße einen 19-jährigen Motorradfahrer. Dieser wurde zum Glück nur leicht verletzt und konnte das Krankenhaus bereits wieder verlassen.

JENNY Well, this one is about shoplifting, isn't it? And there's something about the store detective.

YOU That's right. *Three people stole pullovers from a shop. They attacked the store detective and ran away.*

JENNY Did they catch them?

YOU *Yes, they did.*

JENNY What about the second one? Is it something about a motorbike rider?

YOU *A car was turning left. It hit the motorbike.*

JENNY Was the rider hurt?

YOU *Yes, but he was OK. He didn't have to stay in hospital.*

JENNY And the last one's about a disco. What does '15 PKW von Vandalen' mean?

YOU *PKW is another word for 'car', so that means that vandals damaged 15 cars.*

JENNY Oh, I see now! That happens all the time at the discos near us. Did they get the people who did it?

It says here they got somebody, 'a suspicious person'. But they are looking for more information.

p. 27/8

10 ▶ A vocabulary mind map

On page 149 of your student's book you can find an idea for learning vocabulary. Look at the example carefully. Then use the words in the box below to complete the mind map on 'Advertising'.

> Werbung, Reklame • The papers are full of adverts • an advert
> to advertise (a product, …) • a way of encouraging people to buy or use something
> A big advertising campaign against … • a TV/newspaper advert
> Should there be advertising on TV? • to put an advert in the paper • an ad

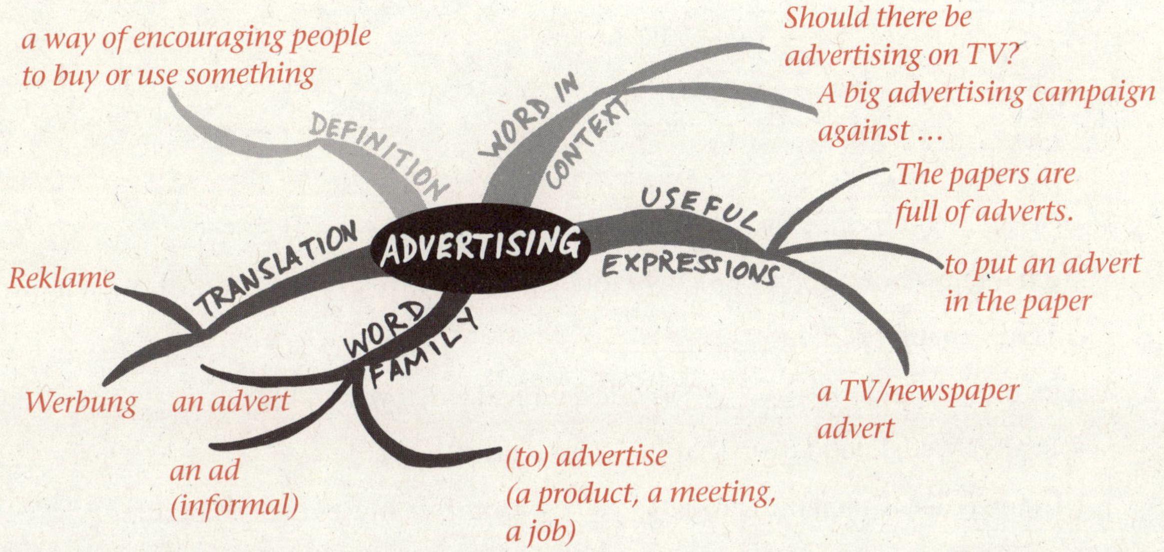

▶▶▶ Now you

In your exercise book, make your own vocabulary mind maps using words from the unit.

p. 28/1

11 ▶ Phrasal verbs

a *Match the sentence halves. Use arrows.*

1 They cut it down
2 I tried it on
3 Mum tried to pick it up
4 I couldn't work it out
5 You should fill it in carefully
6 I think he should give it up
7 We had to divide it up
8 We had to put it up really quickly

but it was too hot.
but I couldn't do the buttons up.
into six pieces.
and send it back to the address at the top.
because he coughs really badly in the mornings.
because it kept too much light out of the garden.
because the rain had started.
because I'm useless at Maths.

b *What might 'it' be in each of the sentences in* **a**? *Write down suggestions in your exercise book.*

c *Complete these sentences in a suitable way. Use phrasal verbs.*

1 There isn't another bus for ages. If I ring my dad, perhaps he'll *pick me up* ________.
2 Coffee is bad for you. I think you should *give it up* ________.
3 There's a great programme on TV right now. Can I *turn it on* ________?
4 I need to find a phone number. Have you got a phone book, so I can *look it up* ________?

p. 29/4

12 ▶ ... test your words

a *Complete these tables:*

VERB	NOUN
attract	attraction
punish	punishment
behave	behaviour
solve	solution

ADJECTIVE	NOUN
free	freedom
violent	violence
legal	law
humorous	humour

b *Complete the sentences. Use word pairs from the tables in* **a**.

1 Mum, I know how to solve my money problems. You give me more pocket money.
– That's an interesting solution.

2 Dad, did you know it's legal to ride a moped when you're 16?
– Really? Well, I don't care what the law says. I say no!

3 This town needs something to attract tourists, a museum or something.
– A big attraction like Alton Towers or the London Eye would be better!

4 I've heard that some very violent people go to football matches.
– Well, I've never seen any violence in our local stadium.

5 I saw some fans on television. Their behaviour was terrible. I hope you and your friends don't behave like that.
– Mum, this is Bedford Rovers, not Manchester United. The fans are all very polite.

6 You've broken the rules. I really should punish you.
– Oh, Dad. I'm a big girl now. What kind of punishment can you give me?

7 That friend of yours has a strange sense of humour. I don't find his jokes funny.
– Really? I find him very humorous. But lots of other people don't laugh either.

8 Mum, I can't wait to get my own flat. I need more freedom.
– Don't forget that being free means doing your washing and paying the bills too!

13 ▶ ... find the odd one out

Make negative adjectives. Then (circle) *the odd one out in each group.*

un happy	in active	(ir regular)	im perfect
un friendly	in correct	un necessary	im possible
(in formal)	in visible	un wanted	(un important)
un kind	(il legal)	un known	im polite

14 ▶ ... give advice in English

How do you say these things in English?

1 Beschäftigt dich irgendetwas? *Is there something on your mind?*

2 Kann ich dir einen Ratschlag geben? *Can I give you a piece of advice?*

3 Du brauchst dich nicht zu schämen. *You needn't feel ashamed.*

4 Ich bin mir sicher, dass du eine Lösung für das Problem findest. *I'm sure you'll find a solution to the problem.*

5 Es ist schließlich nur menschlich, Fehler zu machen. *After all, it's only human to make mistakes.*

6 Verliere nicht den Kontakt zu deinen Freunden. *Don't lose touch with your friends.*

7 Ich schlage vor, dass du mit einem Lehrer sprichst. *I suggest that you talk to a teacher.*

8 Lasse es nicht zu, dass er sich über dich lustig macht. *Don't allow him to make fun of you.*

15 ▶ ... write about your friends

a *What are the best things about your best friends? Are they funny, quick-thinking, interesting, …? Do they have annoying habits too? Are they late for everything? Do they embarrass you? Make notes.*

b *Write a paragraph describing the things you love about them, and the things you hate.*

1 ▶ What did they say?

A reporter spoke to several people in the shopping centre. Complete his report.

I spoke to several people at the shopping centre. One lady mentioned that *she had seen a large group of people the day before.*

A man said that *they were often there and they behaved very badly.*

I also spoke to some teenagers. One girl said that *there were some people who just didn't like teenagers.*

Her friend disagreed. He said that *some of the kids were very rude and they could frighten the old people.*

He added that *they scared him sometimes.*

2 ▶ Talking about school

Use prepositions to complete this conversation.

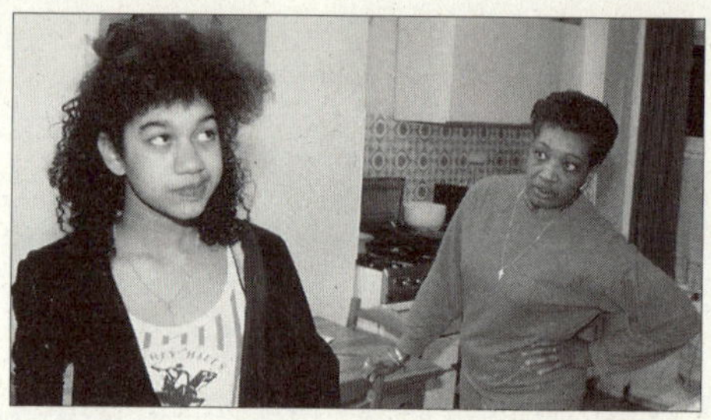

MUM How are you getting on *with* your new French teacher?

KID Well, I was a bit scared *of* him at first. The sister *of* my friend Katie had warned us *about* him. She said he had a very traditional way *of* teaching. He's a specialist *in* 18th century literature. In one lesson he read us an extract *from* his favourite novel and asked us to comment *on* it. It didn't make any sense *to* me! And he wants us to take part *in* a play.

MUM What's wrong *with* that?

KID It's *in* French! And we've got to do a survey *on* teenage interests.

MUM That sounds very interesting *to* me.

KID But I don't care what percentage *of* my class reads magazines! Then he divided us up *into* groups to do the survey. Our group consists *of* me, Katie, Peter and Brian. If you ask Brian a question, he just stares *at* you. What can you do *with* someone like that? I can't work *under* those conditions.

MUM You poor thing!

Computer-Ideen für den Englischunterricht
Das praxisbezogene Handbuch gibt konkrete Anregungen zum Computereinsatz, wie E-Mail, Internet, Lernsoftware. Sie greifen Lehrplan-Themen für die Klassen 5–10 auf. Die beiliegende CD-ROM liefert *web sites,* Textsammlungen und Zusatzinformationen.

Video-Ideen für den Englischunterricht
Von H. Weißling und B. Yareham
Nach methodischen Bereichen gegliedert enthält das *teacher's resource book* Informationen und Tipps zum Einsatz des Mediums Video, dazu praktische Unterrichtsvorschläge, Aufgaben, Kopiervorlagen zu ausgewählten Szenen aus Filmen und Fernsehsendungen und eine Liste geeigneter Videos.

Cornelsen online
Besuchen Sie uns im Internet: Neben dem Online-Katalog mit allen Titeln aus unserem Verlagsprogramm finden Sie hier aktuelle Informationen und viele Angebote zum Herunterladen. Also surfen Sie mal herein, wir haben 24 Stunden für Sie geöffnet:
http://www.cornelsen.de

Bestellkarte

Hiermit bestelle ich zu den ausgewiesenen Abgabebedingungen:

☐ **Handbuch für den Unterricht A5**
Bestellnr. 351700. ☐◇ 32,90 DM

☐ **1 Text-Cassette A5** ca. 75 Min.
Bestellnr. 351769 ◇ 32,90 DM

☐ **2 Text-Cassetten A5** ca. 150 Min.
Bestellnr. 351777 ◇ 49,50 DM

☐ **Leistungsmessung A5 – Heft mit CD**
Bestellnr. 351742 ☐◇ 29,80 DM

☐ **Planet Pinkfast … (Sketche)**
Bestellnr. 61337 ☐◇ 29,80 DM

☐ **Practical English Usage, kartoniert**
Bestellnr. 106080 ◐ 51,50 DM

☐ **Computer-Ideen im Englischunterricht**
Handbuch mit CD-ROM. Bestellnr. 61345 39,80 DM

☐ **Video-Ideen für den Englischunterricht**
Bestellnr. 44980 32,90 DM

☐ **Timm, Englisch lernen und lehren**
Bestellnr. 6190 42,90 DM

☐ **1 Text-CD A5** ca. 75 Min.
Bestellnr. 351939 ◇ 33,90 DM

☐ **2 Text-CDs A5** ca. 150 Min
Bestellnr. 351947 ◇ 53,90 DM

☐ **Leistungsmessung A5 – CD-ROM**
Bestellnr. 914054 ☐◇ 39,— DM

☐ **Right or Wrong?**
Bestellnr. 168212 ◐ 24,90 DM

☐ **Practical English Usage, gebunden**
Bestellnr. 107515 ◐ 69,80 DM

Gewünschtes bitte in dem entsprechenden Kästchen deutlich ankreuzen. Preisstand 1.1.2001. Änderungen vorbehalten. ◐ = zur Prüfung mit 20% Rabatt, ◇ = Unverbindl. Preisempfehlung, ☐ = nur direkt vom Verlag

BK 315

Schulstempel *Bitte in Druckschrift ausfüllen*

Meine Cornelsen Kundennummer:
Bitte bei allen Bestellungen angeben

Name / Vorname

Straße / Hausnummer

Postleitzahl / Ort

Ort / Datum

Unterschrift

Bitte freimachen

Antwortkarte

Cornelsen

Cornelsen Verlag

14328 Berlin

3 ▶ On the beach

Complete the sentences with the correct words from the brackets.

> **tip** Words like *glasses* and *trousers* can only be used in the plural. If you want to talk about one of them, you have to say 'a pair of ...'

DANA I like your sunglasses. (Was it/Were they) *Were they* expensive? Can I try (it/them) *them* on?

ANGIE Of course. Here you are. (That/Those) *Those* shorts you're wearing (is/are) *are* really trendy. Where did you get (it/them) *them*?

DANA In that new shop in town. I had to buy a new (one/pair) *pair* because my old (one/ones) *ones* (was/were) *were* too small. (This/These) *This* T-shirt (is/are) *is* new too. Have you got a bottle of sunscreen? I need (one/some) *some* for my nose.

ANGIE You can keep the bottle. I have to go now. Where (is/are) *are* my trousers? Can you see (it/them) *them*?

DANA There's (one/some) *some* over there. Look, that dog has got (it/them) *them* in its mouth!

4 ▶ A bad day

a *Match the sentence halves.*

1 My brother got up really late,
2 Dad didn't read the washing instructions on his new red tracksuit,
3 My sister spent two hours on the Internet,
4 Her friends are always 'chatting' in chatrooms,
5 Someone stole my bike at the youth club on Saturday night,

- which meant that nobody else could use the phone.
- which they say is good for their English.
- which meant that he was late for school.
- which meant I had to walk home.
- which explains why his white socks are now pink.

(Answers: 1 – which meant that he was late for school. 2 – which explains why his white socks are now pink. 3 – which meant that nobody else could use the phone. 4 – which they say is good for their English. 5 – which meant I had to walk home.)

b *Finish these sentences. Use* non-defining relative clauses.

1 I got home really late on Saturday, which *means that I'm not allowed out all this week.*

2 My mobile is broken, which *means that I can't send text messages at the moment.*

3 My friend got her nose pierced, which *looks cool, but I wouldn't do it.*

4 I ate too much last night, which *explains why I feel sick this morning.*

3 Up North in Yorkshire

1 ▶ What does ... make you think of?

Write a paragraph like the ones on pages 30/31 of your student's book, describing a region of Germany. You don't have to know the region well. Just describe what it makes you think of.

- Is there a favourite expression people use in/about the region? What does it mean? Is it true?
- Is there anything special about the history of this region, its geography or its people?

When I think of Swabia I think of the expression 'Schaffe, schaffe, Häusle baue', which means 'Work hard and build your own house'. The people of Swabia like to think they work very hard. I think the people are very generous and friendly. The other thing I think of is the countryside, which is so beautiful.

p. 31

2 Blue box It's an 'either-or' situation → blue box, p. 150

Write one sentence instead of two, using the words in brackets.

1 We're going on holiday. We might go to Yorkshire or we might go to New York. *(either … or …)*

We're going either to Yorkshire or to New York on holiday.

2 Mum hasn't been to New York. Dad hasn't been to New York. *(neither … nor…)*

Neither Mum nor Dad have been to New York.

3 Mum thinks a trip to New York would be expensive. She also thinks it would be tiring. *(both … and …)*

Mum thinks a trip to New York would be both expensive and tiring.

4 She says walking in the Yorkshire Dales is more relaxing. It's also a lot cheaper. *(not only …, but also …)*

She says walking in the Yorkshire Dales is not only more relaxing, but also a lot cheaper.

5 My sister wants to go to New York. I want to go there too. *(both … and …)*

Both my sister and I want to go to New York.

6 Mum can't decide what to do. Dad can't decide either. *(neither … nor…)*

Neither Mum nor Dad can decide what to do.

p. 31

3 ▶ Formal and informal words

a *Complete the list with words and phrases that mean the same, but are more neutral or formal. The words are all in the word box.*

J	K	A	U	O	A	C	K	T	H	W	E	E	G	P	P	E	I
U	C	F	D	J	W	A	L	H	O	W	E	V	E	R	O	Y	N
T	S	O	L	V	I	N	F	O	R	M	R	E	F	U	S	E	V
R	W	R	M	W	E	H	V	T	S	R	D	R	R	S	S	A	I
E	Q	B	L	M	L	R	E	I	E	E	O	F	R	A	I	T	S
A	I	I	K	L	I	E	T	S	L	R	G	H	R	H	B	Q	I
E	N	D	A	W	G	T	A	B	C	Z	A	H	I	I	L	U	B
X	V	C	M	N	M	L	A	R	A	Z	P	L	L	R	E	I	L
P	E	C	A	J	K	Y	P	C	T	A	R	T	L	R	A	N	E
R	N	R	Z	L	O	O	R	K	R	W	S	T	O	P	F	T	D
E	T	T	I	J	M	U	S	A	D	I	R	E	C	T	F	E	E
S	M	Z	N	E	R	T	P	T	J	T	M	F	O	B	E	R	N
S	J	E	G	T	W	H	V	T	H	E	R	E	F	O	R	E	D

1 to say no = *refuse*
2 but = *however*
3 mate = *friend*
4 give up = *stop*
5 ad = *advert*
6 to tell sb. = *inform*
7 doable = *possible*
8 fun = *enjoyable*
9 weird = *strange*
10 so = *therefore*
11 think up = *invent*
12 Wow! = That's *amazing* .
13 down-to-earth = *direct*
14 Stay cool! = Keep *calm* .
15 in the end = *after all*
16 You can't see it. = It's *invisible* .
17 Do it up! = *Close* it!
18 when she was a girl = in her *youth*
19 You can't do that! = I *forbid* you to do that!
20 to do something wrong = *commit a crime*
21 to say or write something = *express*
22 to say sth. in different words = *paraphrase*

b *Write these sentences in a more formal way. Use words from* **a**.

1 Just a note to tell you that I have to say no to your invitation.

I'm writing to *inform you that I have to refuse your invitation.*

2 It's such a pain! Dad has said that I can't go out.

I'm afraid my father *has forbidden me to go out.*

3 It was hard to say no. I had to think up an excuse.

It was hard to refuse to do it. I had to invent an excuse.

c *Write this note in a more informal way.*

It was an amazing weekend. I kept calm and in the end my father allowed me to go out. Lisa's friends are rather strange. However, the party was very enjoyable.

Wow! What a weekend! I stayed cool and Dad let me go after all. Lisa's mates are weird, but the party was great fun.

p. 33/3

4 ▶ A walk to remember

Prepare to write about the best – or the worst! – walk you've done. Perhaps it was a tough walk like the Three Peaks Challenge, or perhaps it was something more relaxed.

a *Complete this mindmap for your walk. You may find some useful words on pages 32/33.*

b *Then write about your walk in your exercise book. Think about the style of your report*
– *short and formal, writing only about the facts*
– *informal, with more information about feelings and positive/negative experiences.*

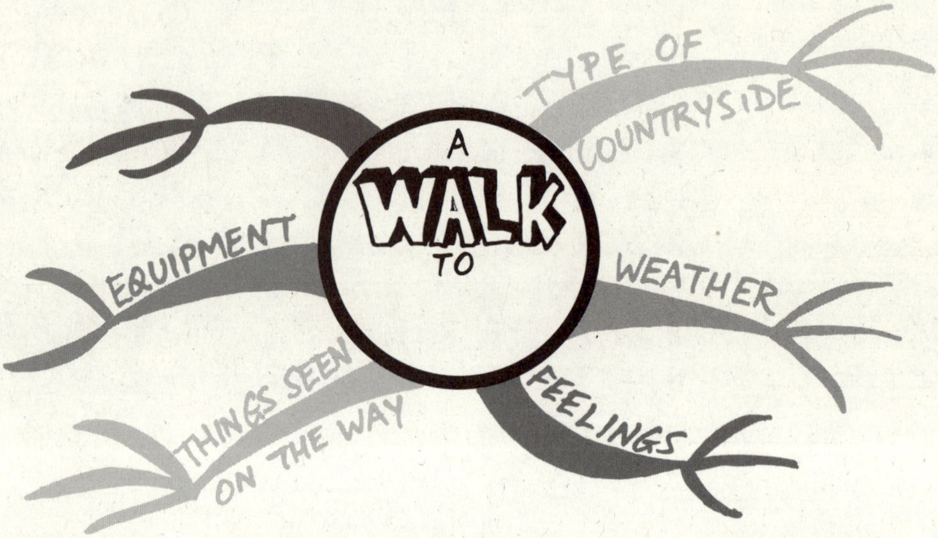

p. 33/3

5 ▶ Word building

a *Make adjectives from the words in the box and complete the table.*

action • anger • attraction • beauty • break • care • create • do • enjoy • fun • hand • industry • life • muck • nature • notice • politics • society • success • use

-al	-y	-ful	-ive	-able
industrial	angry	beautiful	active	breakable
natural	funny	careful	attractive	doable
political	handy	successful	creative	enjoyable
social	lively	useful		noticeable
	mucky			

b *Using what you know about word building, explain the underlined words in these sentences.*

1 She really is a destructive child. — *The child destroys everything.*
2 Your work has improved noticeably. — *I can notice the improvement.*
3 He gave me a meaningful look. — *He said it with his look, not words.*
4 Careful with that glass! It is breakable, you know. — *It can break easily.*
5 I've got sweaty socks. — *The socks are wet with sweat.*
6 The list of words is alphabetical. — *The words go from A to Z.*

p. 33/3

6 ▶ From a brochure

Complete the text of this brochure. Use participle forms of the verbs in brackets.

New Lanark Mills, Scotland

(found) *Founded* in 1785, New Lanark Mills soon became a successful business. By 1793 there were four mills, all (power) *powered* by water wheels. Of the 1157 people (employ) *employed* at the mills, only 362 were adults, the rest (be) *being* young boys and girls.

New Lanark's most famous owner was Robert Owen. (work) *Having worked* in the textile business all his life, he had developed his own ideas about how to treat his workers. He wanted to improve housing and working conditions, (believe) *believing* that better conditions would make the workers more efficient. His education system, (begin) *begun* in 1816, was very modern, (encourage) *encouraging* subjects like singing, dancing and nature study.

(stop) *Having stopped* production in 1968, the mills were bought by new owners in 1974. (realize) *Realizing* the potential of the mills for tourism, they built a visitor centre. New Lanark Mills is now very successful, (attract) *attracting* half a million people every year. A very popular attraction is a ride that shows what life was like in the Industrial Revolution, (recreate) *recreating* the experiences of a 19th century mill worker.

▶▶▶ Now you

Write about a tourist attraction near you. Describe its history and what is on offer there. Use as many participle forms as possible.

____

____

____

____

_______________ p. 37/4

7 ▶ Young people and work

Translate this text in your exercise book.

The European Parliament has criticized Britain for allowing teenagers between the ages of 13 and 16 to do part-time jobs. The Parliament in Strasbourg believes that by taking on paid part-time jobs, young people's health, education and general welfare will suffer and wants EU governments to set the minimum working age at 16.

In Britain, more than two million schoolchildren are involved in a huge number of different part-time jobs. The most popular ways of earning extra pocket money are early-morning paper rounds, 'Saturday jobs' as shop assistants, fruit-picking, milk rounds, catering and babysitting. The British government believes it's good to get a taste of work at an early age. Young people get experience of the workplace and society, they learn to handle money, they gain a sense of independence and self-respect.

- 43 % of schoolchildren between the ages of 13 and 17 work in some form of employment in the UK.
- The UK has the highest percentage in Europe of working 13- and 14-year-olds – around 30 %.
- Under UK law, teenagers between the ages of 13 and 16 are allowed to work two hours a day on school days, only one of which can be before school. At weekends or during holidays, you can work for up to five hours a day at ages 13 and 14, and for up to eight hours a day at ages 15 and 16.

▶▶▶ Now you

Who do you agree with – the British government or the European Parliament, and why?

____

____

____

____ p. 38/7

8 ▶ Past, present and future

a *Put the words and phrases in a suitable place on the diagram.*

a fortnight ago • all the time • at the moment • every day • in an hour
in the 1600s • in the last century • in years to come • ~~next month~~ • now
over the last ten years • the day after tomorrow • ~~the day before yesterday~~ • yesterday

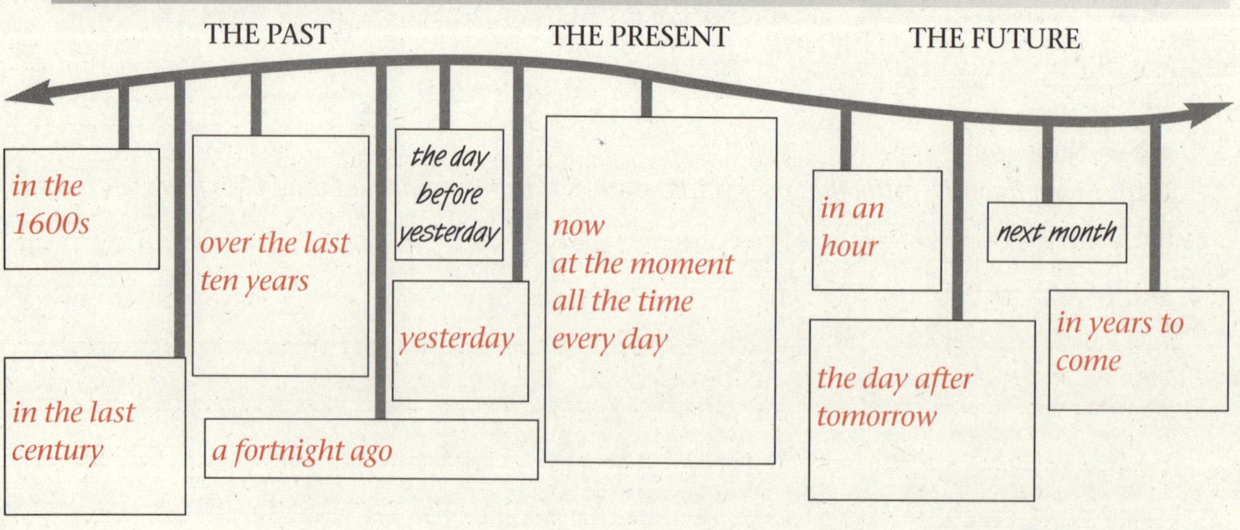

b *Complete this look into the future, putting the verbs in brackets in the correct tense.*

What (happen) <u>*will happen*</u> in the next 50 years? (change) <u>*Will*</u> our lives <u>*change*</u> a lot? Or (be) <u>*will*</u> the 21st century <u>*be*</u> a lot like the 20th century? In the past people (be) <u>*were*</u> very afraid of the word 'cancer'. But doctors say that in the future they (have) <u>*will have*</u> better ways of helping people with illnesses like these. They say that the next generation (know) <u>*will know*</u> more about the dangers of smoking and the importance of good food. Experts expect that more people (become) <u>*will become*</u> vegetarian, and people (ask) <u>*will ask*</u> more questions about how their food is produced. The next ten years (be) <u>*will be*</u> a very exciting time for space travel. By 2010 we (know) <u>*will know*</u> if there is life on Mars. Our climate (change) <u>*is changing*</u> at the moment. Already some parts of the world (have) <u>*have*</u> too much water and others (not have) <u>*don't have*</u> enough. If we (want) <u>*want*</u> to stop climate change, we (have to) <u>*will have to*</u> use more alternative energy than we do now. In the last 20 years technology (change) <u>*has changed*</u> our world a lot. In the eighties we (get) <u>*got*</u> computers. In the nineties it (be) <u>*was*</u> the Internet. In the 21st century we (see) <u>*will see*</u> other exciting developments. For example some people predict that in 50 years cars (fly) <u>*will fly*</u>.

▶▶▶ Now you

Read the text in **b** *again. Do you agree with the predictions made by the experts? For example, will doctors beat cancer? Will people become vegetarian? Will scientists find life on Mars? Will cars fly? Write about what you think.*

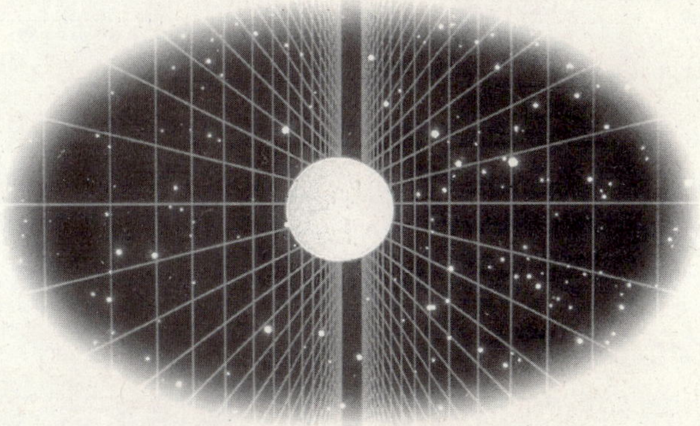

I hope that doctors will beat cancer. A lot of my friends are already vegetarian, but I don't think people will stop smoking. I don't think they'll find life on Mars either. I'm sure people will try to use more alternative energy. But I don't think the problem of climate change will be solved. I'm sure more people will use computers, but I don't think we'll have flying cars in the next 50 years.

p. 41/4

9 ▶ ... use these words correctly

a *Complete the sentences with the correct words from the box.*

discover invent	1 James Watt invented the steam engine. Alexander Fleming discovered penicillin.
remember remind	2 I mustn't forget to ring my mother. How am I going to remember? – Don't worry. I'll remind you.
fair fairly	3 I'm fairly good at chess: I beat Susan. – OK, but are you a fair player?
guest host	4 The guest is the visitor, and the host is the person who welcomes the visitor.
certainly surely	5 It's certainly an interesting place. You don't want to go already, surely?

b *Write sentences that show the difference between these pairs of words.*

rob	He robbed a bank and an old lady,
steal	and then stole some games from a shop.
so	That house is so big!
such	It's such a big house that 100 people could live in it.
handy	Remember this handy advice.
mobile	Can I phone you on your mobile?

10 ▶ ... get the stress right

Say these words and decide where the stress is. Put them into the correct list. Check your answers in the dictionary.

biography • compass • conditions • conflict (n.) • detective
district • economy • efficient • humour • industrial
machinery • natural • neutral • official • photographer
potential • private • quality • region • vandalism

on the first syllable as in 'politics'		on the second syllable as in 'production'	
compass	neutral	biography	industrial
conflict	private	conditions	machinery
district	quality	detective	official
humour	region	economy	photographer
natural	vandalism	efficient	potential

12 ▶ ... talk about a place

How do you say these things in English?

1 Ich würde gern die hässlichen Hochhäuser loswerden.

I'd love to get rid of the ugly high-rise buildings.

2 Ich würde sie durch Wohnsiedlungen ersetzen.

I'd replace them with housing estates.

3 Das Stadtzentrum ist immer voll mit Leuten.

The city centre is always crowded with people.

4 Für diese Gegend gibt es viele Möglichkeiten.

This area has a lot of potential.

5 Die Arbeitslosigkeit ist ein großes Problem.

Unemployment is a major problem.

6 Man kann dahin einen Tagesausflug machen.

You can go there for a day out.

7 Sie sind wegen der Pläne wütend.

They're up in arms about the plans.

8 Ich gebe den Planern die Schuld.

I blame the planners.

12 ▶ ... write about a place you know

a *Prepare to write about a place you know that needs some changes. First think about what is good about the place. Then think about the things you'd like to change. Make notes on a mind map.*

b *Write your text.*

4 Fáilte – Welcome to Ireland

1 ▶ The Irish language

Read this chatroom discussion about Irish. Then write a comment in your exercise book.

Fáilte

[Jane has entered the chat]

Laura: Kids in Germany are lucky. My German penfriend started learning English ages ago and now she's really good at it. I'm useless at German, but I was 13 before I started to learn it.

Jane: Yes, but we learn Irish from the age of four. That's important too. It's part of our culture. It's part of what's special about Ireland and being Irish.

Laura: So what? It doesn't help me get a job!

Jane: But don't you think that it's important to keep the Irish language alive? I do.

Laura: The truth is that the real language of Ireland is English. Only 4% of the population speaks Irish regularly at home – but we still have to spend years learning it at school. French and German – or Russian or Chinese – would be much more useful.

Jane: I'm afraid you're mixing up two separate things here. Of course it's important to learn languages, but we have to protect the Irish language too. If people don't learn it at school, they'll never learn it. Does anybody else have a view on this? If you were Irish, would you want to learn Irish?

p. 45/3

2 ▶ At a summer camp

Imagine that you and an Italian girl, Gina, are responsible for a group of little children at a summer camp. Complete these dialogues.

tip If you don't know a word, paraphrase!

a GINA Look at little Kevin. He's crying. You'll have to talk to him. You speak German, I don't.

YOU *Kevin, was ist los? Warum weinst du?*

KEVIN Ich habe seit drei Tagen keine Post von zu Hause.

YOU He says *he hasn't had post from home for 3 days .*

GINA Tell him to calm down. We'll go to the reception. If there's no post for him, he can phone home from there.

YOU *Beruhige dich, Kevin. Gina meint, wir gehen jetzt zur Rezeption.*
Wenn da keine Post für dich ist, kannst du von dort aus zu Hause anrufen.

KEVIN Das ist nett von euch, aber ich weiß nicht die Vorwahl für Deutschland.

YOU *He says he doesn't know the number you have to put in front (international code) for Germany.*

GINA Oh, do you know it? If not, we can find out at the reception.

YOU Okay. Kevin, kein Problem. *Wir fragen an der Rezeption.*

b GINA Kevin's crying again. You'd better see what's the matter.

KEVIN Ich habe Heimweh.

YOU *He says he's sad because he's missing his family (he is homesick).*

GINA Tell him I've got some special sweets that will make him feel better.

YOU *Gina hat Spezialbonbons, die dagegen helfen.*

KEVIN Ja, wirklich?

p. 45/3

3 ▶ A letter home

Complete the letter with phrases from the box.

and yet • besides • by the time
by the way • eventually • in case
nothing but • rather than

Dear Mum and Dad,

Having a terrible time. The food is absolutely awful. I expect I'll be dead by the time *you get this letter. And* by the way*, that walkman you got me is useless. I've had* nothing but *trouble with it all week.*

There's nothing to do here in the evenings. I sometimes go to the céilíthe, but they're boring. Besides*, I hate dancing. I did go to one last night. I wasn't brave enough to ask someone to dance, but* eventually *this girl asked me. She was really small and light,* and yet *she was a really terrible dancer, just like me! We decided it was safer to chat* rather than *dance. We got on quite well together.*

There was another fire alarm last night. They say we have to know what to do in case *there's a fire. But I'm so tired that if there is a fire, I won't wake up.*

See you on Friday.

p. 45/3

4 ▶ Your favourite artist

Ian James admired singer-songwriter Juliet Turner so much that he designed a website about her! (Juliet Turner is from Omagh, Northern Ireland and appears on the CD 'Across the Bridge of Hope'.)

a *Read what Ian writes about Juliet Turner, then think about these questions:*
If you were going to design a website for your favourite musician or group, who would you choose? Why do you admire this person/group? What is special about them for you?

Juliet Turner

Back Forward Reload Home Search Netscape Images Print Security Stop

Location: http://web.ukonline.co.uk/juliet.turner/ What's Related

juliet turner

[news] [concerts] [what's new] [CDs] [pics]

welcome

I first saw Juliet Turner at the Greenbelts Arts Festival. I hadn t planned to see her, but she came on and played one or two songs. I was really impressed by her voice that was strong and soft at the same time, by her presence, and by songs that were so obviously from the heart, full of the joy and pain of life. Afterwards I bought a copy of her album, Let s Hear it for Pizza (see CDs) and I have never tired of it yet. Ian

b *Write a short text about your favourite artist/group.*

p. 46/2

5 Revision All about food

a *Put the verbs in brackets in the correct active or passive form.*

At the beginning of the 20th century, farmers (start) started to change the way they produce food and shops (begin) began to sell different products. Between 1901 and 1905, US wheat fields (cut) were cut with machines for the first time, instant coffee (invent) was invented, and Coca-Cola (sell) was sold in Britain for the first time. In 1916 the first supermarket (open) (was) opened. At the beginning of the century, chicken (be) was a luxury for most people. But later, chickens (produce) were produced in huge numbers and it (become) became a cheap meat. In 1945 the microwave (invented) was invented and people (spend) spent less time in the kitchen. Some New York apartments (build) are built without kitchens now because some people (not, want) don't want to cook at all.

b *Use the notes to answer these questions. Use the passive.*

1 I love potatoes. How can I cook them quickly? (can/cook – 4 minutes – microwave)
Potatoes can be cooked in 4 minutes in the microwave.

2 How long should I boil eggs so they are completely safe? (must/boil – at least 5 minutes)
Eggs must be boiled at least 5 minutes.

3 I hate finding insects in my salad. How can I get it completely clean? (should/wash – water – salt in it)
Salad should be washed in water with salt in it.

4 How long can I keep fish in the fridge? (must/use – the day you buy it)
Fish must be used the day you buy it.

5 Should I keep my vegetables in the fridge? (can/keep – the fridge – or – cool, dark cupboard)
Vegetables can be kept in the fridge or in a cool, dark cupboard.

6 ▶ Make your own networks

Don't forget that networks are a very useful way to collect and learn vocabulary. Copy and complete this network in your exercise book – or better still, design your own.

tip Keep adding to your networks when you meet new words from these word fields.

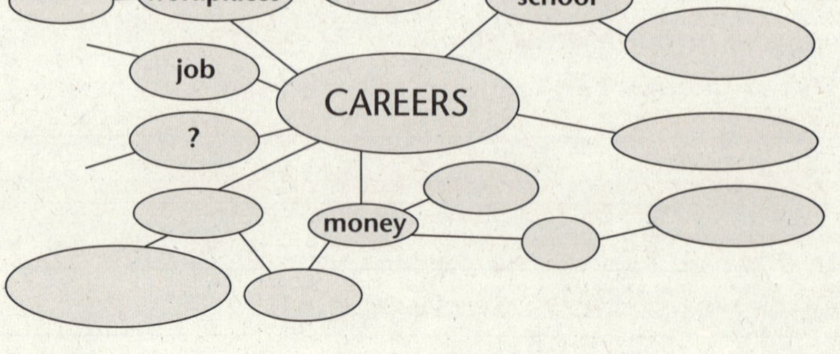

p. 49/3

7 ▶ That's what I was told

a *Rewrite these sentences. Use the passive. Begin with the underlined part.*

1 Someone sent me a brochure on recycling rubbish.
I was sent a brochure on recycling rubbish.

2 Someone told me that Ireland is worried about pollution.
I was told that Ireland was worried about pollution.

3 One of our teachers asked us to bring our bikes to school today.
We were asked to bring our bikes to school today.

4 Someone invited us to visit an organic farm .
We were invited to visit an organic farm.

5 They gave me some organic apples.
I was given some organic apples.

6 They never offer students vegetarian food in the school canteen.
Students are never offered vegetarian food in the school canteen.

7 They teach students not to waste water.
Students are taught not to waste water.

b *Finish these sentences.*

1 For my birthday I was given ____________________

2 Yesterday I was asked ____________________

3 I was invited ____________________

p. 49/5

8 ▶ Expressions with *keep*, *make* and *take*

a *Which words in the box can go with these verbs? Complete the table.*

alive • busy • calm • contact with sb.
a date • dry • an exam • fit • friends
a guess • music • over • part in • peace
photos • a point • power
sb./sth. seriously • a speech • steps
up a challenge • warm

keep	*alive, busy, calm, contact with sb., a date, dry, fit, warm*
make	*contact with sb., a date, friends, music, peace, a point, a speech*
take	*an exam, a guess, over, part in, power, s.o./s.th. seriously, steps, up a challenge*

b *Choose three expressions from each list. In your exercise book write sentences that are true for you.*
Example: *I like to make music with my friends. I make friends easily.*

p. 49/5

9 ▶ More on phrasal verbs

Phrasal verbs often have more than one meaning, so when you look them up in a dictionary, you have to read the whole entry carefully.

go off **1** to leave a place, especially in order to do sth: *She went off to get a drink.* **2** to be fired; to explode: *The gun went off by accident.* **3** if an ALARM goes off, it makes a sudden loud noise **4** if a light, etc. goes off, it stops working: *The heating goes off at night.* **5** *(BrE, informal)* to fall asleep: *Hasn't the baby gone off yet?* **6** *(BrE)* if food or drink goes off, it become bad and not fit to eat or drink. **7** *(BrE)* to get worse in quality: *Her books have gone off in recent years.* **8 go off sb/sth** *(BrE, informal)* to stop liking sb/sth or lose interest in them: *I've gone off beer.*

a *Match the underlined verbs in these sentences with the correct meaning in the dictionary entry.*

1 …, so I wanted to get up early but the alarm didn't go off. I wonder … *3*
2 … used to love Britney Spears, but he's gone off her now. Now … *8*
3 … you going? You can't just go off like that. You have to help me … *1*
4 … terrible smell in the fridge. I think that meat has gone off. I told you … *6*
5 … I thought he'd never go off , but in the end he stopped crying. I was so … *5*

b *Write a suitable beginning and ending for the sentences in* **a** *in your exercise book.*
Example: *I promised my friend that I'd catch the early bus, so I wanted to get up early but the alarm didn't go off. I wonder if he's mad with me.*

c *You already know one meaning of these phrasal verbs. But they have other meanings too. Study the dictionary entries, then complete these sentences.*

pick up **1** to get better, stronger, etc.; to improve: *Granny is picking up again after her illness.* **2** *(informal)* to start again; to continue: *Let's pick up where we stopped yesterday.* **pick sb/sth up** **1** to take hold of sb/sth and lift them/it up **2** to get an electronic signal, sound or picture: *We were able to pick up the BBC World Service.*

do sth up **1** to fasten a coat, skirt, etc.: *He never does his jacket up.* **2** *(BrE)* to repair and decorate a house,etc.: *He makes money by buying old houses and doing them up.* **do yourself up** **1** *(informal)* to make yourself more attractive by putting on make-up, attractive clothes, etc.

get on with sb to have a friendly relationship with sb: *She's never really got on with her sister.* **get on with sth** **1** used to talk about how well sb is doing a task **2** to continue doing sth, especially after an interruption

1 My parents bought a really old house. They had to *do* it *up* before we could live in it.
2 OK, you lot. Stop talking now and *get on with* your Maths.
3 The weather isn't very good today, but I think it will *pick up* tomorrow.
4 Before my older brother goes out, he spends ages in the bathroom. He likes to *do* himself *up* .
5 What radio stations can you *pick up* on your new radio?

p. 50/2

10 ▶ In the Name of the Father

In the Name of the Father *is a film that was based on Gerry Conlon's book 'Proven Innocent'. It was very successful, but also attracted some criticism. Read this review.*

In the Name of the Father is a great film. It got a lot of criticism, especially in Britain. People said it was pro-IRA and that it didn't tell the true story. But this a drama and not a news report, so sometimes the director had to change things a bit. But he never lets us forget that although what happened to Conlon was not right, the bomb in Guildford was also a terrible act. And this is the shocking image that we first see on the screen. *(RTE Guide)*

▶▶▶ Now you

Think of a film that you know that was based on a true story or on historical events, for example The Patriot *or* Pearl Harbor. *How important do you think it is that films tell the facts and only the facts? Or do you agree with the writer of this review that a film director can change things a bit if it makes a better film? Express your opinion in your exercise book.*

p. 51/2

11 ▶ How much do you know?

a *Circle the correct answers and label the map.*

tip You might find it useful to look at the map at the front of your student's book.

1 Great Britain is
- a England and Wales
- (b) England, Scotland and Wales
- c England, Scotland, Wales and Northern Ireland

2 The United Kingdom is
- a England and Wales
- b England, Scotland and Wales
- (c) England, Scotland, Wales and Northern Ireland

3 The British Isles include
- a England, Scotland and Wales
- b England, Scotland, Wales and Northern Ireland
- (c) England, Scotland, Wales and the island of Ireland

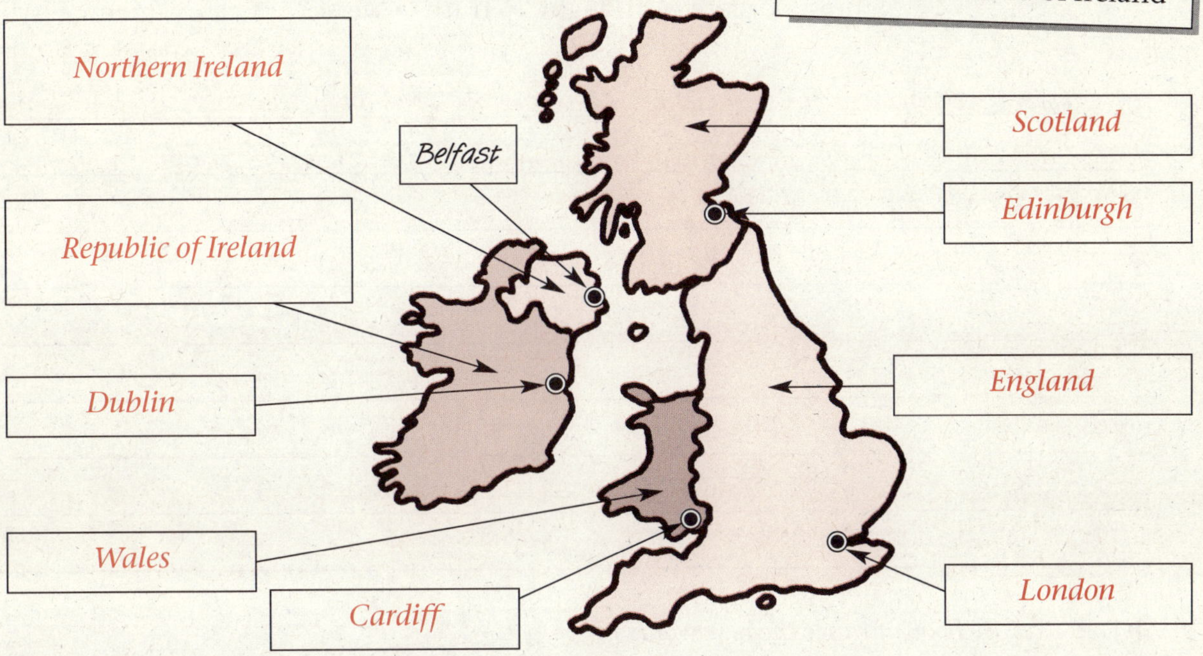

b *Complete this timeline of Irish history.*

1690	1795	1801	*1921*	*1968*	1998
Battle of the Boyne: William of Orange beat James II	Beginning of the Orange Order	*Ireland became part of UK*	Ireland divided into two parts – Northern Ireland and the 'Free State'	Civil rights marches in Northern Ireland	*Good Friday Agreement, Omagh bomb*

c *Answer these questions.*

1 Who are the 'Loyalists' in Northern Ireland loyal to? *Britain/The Queen*

2 Which 'nation' is important for the Nationalists in Northern Ireland?

Republic of Ireland.

3 When people talk about the '32 Counties', what do they mean?

The whole of the island of Ireland.

4 What are these letters short for?

*I*rish *R*epublican *A*rmy. *R*oyal *U*lster *C*onstabulary.

p. 53/5

12 ▶ ... make new words

a *Look at the chart below. Add a prefix, or a suffix – or both – to the basic words and see how many new words you can make.*
Make spelling changes if necessary, e.g. act + ive + ity = activity.
Check your words in a dictionary.

Prefixes	Basic words	Suffixes
un- • dis- re- • ex- op- • co-	accept • act • agree • announce • appear change • dependent • employ • help • honest major • mind • operate • place • port press • state • thought • truth • verse	-able • -ence -er • -ful -ion • -ity • -ive -ment • -y

(un)acceptable, action, actor, react, reaction, disagree/able, agreement, agreeable, announcement, disappear, changeable, exchange, employer, employment, unemployment, helpful, honesty, dishonest/y, majority, remind, reminder, mindful, cooperate, cooperation, replace, replacement, report, export, reporter, express/ion, repress/ion, oppress/ion, statement, thoughtful, un/truthful, version, reverse

b *In your exercise book, arrange the new words in different groups. For example, you could put all the adjectives in one list, all the verbs in another etc. Or you could put together all the words that come from the same basic word. Or you could use mind maps.*

adjectives	verbs	nouns
acceptable active	react	action

13 ▶ ... get it right

Some words behave differently in English and this can cause problems for German speakers. Complete these sentences.

1 My teacher gave me some useful (*Ratschläge*) advice/ pieces of advice.

2 I'll be ready in a minute. I've got to brush my (*Haare*) hair.

3 Oh no! I've got another hole in my (*Hose*) trousers.

4 I've got (*eine schlechte Nachricht*) some/ a bit of bad news.

Vandals got into the school.

5 They sprayed some walls and broke some (*Möbel*) furniture in the headteacher's room.

6 We haven't got any (*Beweise*) proof, but we have an idea who did it.

7 The police are on the phone. They have some new (*Informationen*) information.

14 ▶ ... talk about politics

How do you say these things in English?

1 Eine neue Präsidentin ist an der Macht.

A new president is in power.

2 Sie wurde mit einer großen Mehrheit gewählt.

She was elected by a large majority.

Irish President Mary McAleese

4 Kein Bürger/Keine Bürgerin darf diskriminiert werden.

No citizen must be discriminated against.

6 Die beiden Seiten haben eine Vereinbarung erreicht.

The two sides have reached an agreement.

3 Die Region hat viele Naturkatastrophen erlitten.

The region has suffered a lot of natural disasters.

5 Eine Untersuchung vom Problem hat angefangen.

An investigation into the problem has started.

15 ▶ ... write about an experience you have had

Prepare to write about a trip where you had to speak another language, perhaps at a summer camp, on a school exchange, or on a school trip, or on holiday.

a *Before you start, look at page 45 of your student's book and read Mide's report again. Think about these questions:* What did you think the trip was going to be like before you went? Were you right? What was your biggest problem? What were the high points? Who did you especially like/dislike? What was the last day like?

b *Make some notes, then write your report in an informal way, in a similar way to Mide's.*

5 Australia – Great Southern Land

1 ▶ Quiz questions

a *Answer these questions about Australia.*

tip It might be useful to look at the map at the back of your student's book when you're doing this quiz.

1. The abbreviation for Australia in Web addresses.
2. Ayers Rock, which is the famous rock in the centre of Australia, has another name. What is it?
3. Where will you find Bondi Beach, the famous Australian surfing beach that you see in many films and TV programmes – Sydney, Alice Springs or Canberra?
4. What is Aussie Rules?
5. What is the capital of Queensland – Perth, Darwin or Brisbane?
6. What is the name of the building in Sydney Harbour that looks a bit like an old sailing ship – the Harbour Bridge or the Opera House?
7. What is the name of the salt-water crocodiles that are found in Australia?
8. An animal from the small island south of Australia (NOT an angel! See page 36 of your workbook.)
9. What is the capital of Australia?

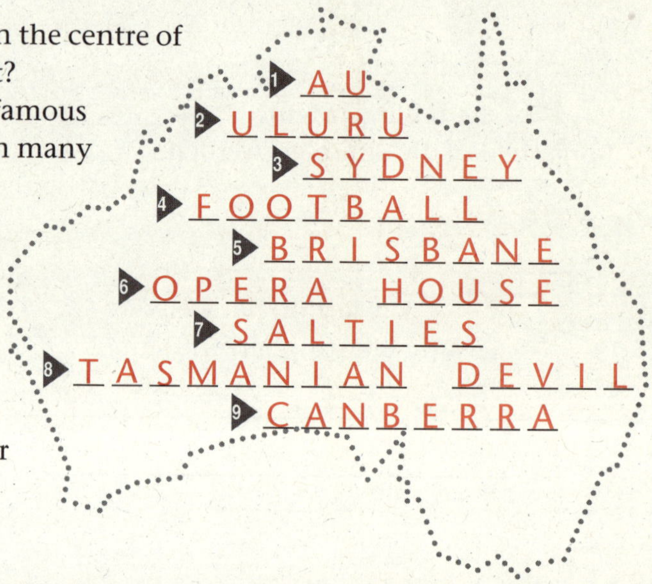

b *Now practise making your own quiz questions. You can use the information in the box if you like.*

FACTS ABOUT AUSTRALIA

- THE POPULATION OF AUSTRALIA IS 18 MILLION. THERE ARE 150 MILLION SHEEP IN AUSTRALIA.
- KANGAROOS DON'T RUN, THEY JUMP, BUT THEY CAN REACH ALMOST 40 KM/H THIS WAY.
- AUSTRALIA IS THE WORLD'S SIXTH LARGEST COUNTRY. IT IS ALMOST AS BIG AS EUROPE.
- 94% OF THE AUSTRALIAN POPULATION IS OF EUROPEAN DESCENT, 4% ASIAN AND 1.5% ABORIGINAL.
- MOST NEW IMMIGRANTS TO AUSTRALIA COME FROM ASIA, ESPECIALLY CHINA AND VIETNAM.
- AUSTRALIA'S NATIONAL DAY IS 26TH JANUARY. CANBERRA IS THE CAPITAL OF AUSTRALIA, BUT IT ISN'T THE BIGGEST CITY. THAT'S SYDNEY.
- KOALAS AREN'T BEARS. THEY ARE A SPECIAL KIND OF ANIMAL CALLED 'MARSUPIALS'. ALL MARSUPIALS CARRY THEIR BABIES IN A KIND OF POCKET.

Which of these animals is not a marsupial?
a) koala b) salty c) kangaroo

How fast can kangaroos go?

What percentage of Australia's population is Aboriginal?
a) less than 5% b) 5 % c) 15%?

Name the biggest city in Australia.

How many sheep are there in Australia?
a) 5 million b) 15 million c) 150 million

p. 55

2 ▶ What's going on?

Speculate about what's going on in one or more of these photos. The phrases in the box might be useful.

> Perhaps/Probably/Maybe … • It's possible that … • may/might
> I think / I'm sure … • The fact that … must mean that …
> The people appear/seem to be …ing…, so I think …

In the first picture, the people look like they are going to a sports event. Perhaps it's a football match; there are only men in the picture. They seem to be happy, but I think they also look a little bit violent. In the second picture, I'm sure the people are also watching sport. The fact that they all look really happy could mean that somebody has just won a race. Perhaps it was Cathy Freeman. In the third picture, the posters must be about the referendum on the monarchy. I know that some people wanted a president, but they wanted the people to vote for him or her, not the politicians.

p.56/1

3 ▶ A rescue

This German tourist has just been rescued by an Australian driver after his car broke down in the outback. He wants to talk to the Australian. Interpret. Use for + noun/pronoun + to-infinitive.

1 Sag ihr, dass ich einen Fehler gemacht habe, indem ich ohne zusätzlichen Benzin losgefahren bin.

It was a mistake *for him to set off without extra petrol*.

2 Sag ihr, dass ich warten muss, bis die Werkstatt ihm Benzin gebracht hat.

He has to wait *for the garage to bring him some petrol*.

3 Frag sie, ob sie dafür sorgen könnte, dass jemand ihm etwas zu trinken gibt.

Can you arrange *for someone to give him something to drink*?

4 Sag ihr, dass es für mich eine Möglichkeit ist, mit einer echten Australierin zu reden.

He says that this is a chance *for him to talk to a real Australian*.

5 Frag sie, warum das Volk dafür gestimmt hat, dass das Land seine Verbindung zur Krone behält.

He wants to know why Australians voted *for the country to keep its link with the Crown*.

p.57/2

4 ▶ The Tasmanians

a *Scan the text below as quickly as you can and decide what it's about. Underline the right answer:*
1 Discovering Australia 2 Holidays in Tasmania 3 Tasmanian Aborigines

A new discovery

In 1642 Abel Tasman discovered an island off the south coast of Australia. He was the first European there and he called it Van Diemen's Land. It was a hilly island covered in dense forest of pine, beech and eucalyptus. Most of the weird marsupials of the Australian mainland were present in Tasmania, including kangaroos, wallabies and duck-billed platypuses. There were also creatures found nowhere else, such as the Tasmanian Devil, which looked like a long-haired bear, and the Tasmanian Tiger, which looked like a great striped dog. But most important for this story, there was also a completely unique race of human beings. They were culturally and ethnically different from the Aborigines of the Australian mainland. They lived in isolated camps in the forests of their remote island, and lived off the wildlife. Nobody knows how many of the original Tasmanians existed when Abel Tasman discovered the island – maybe a few thousand.

A British colony

For more than a century the Europeans weren't interested in the island. But in 1803 the British claimed the island and decided to use it as a prison and send convicts there. By 1820 there were European settlements at both ends of the island, and by 1840 there were more free settlers than convicts.

Cruel times

At first the Aborigines were friendly to the white colonists. But the settlers wanted land. They regarded the Aborigines as enemies, and pushed them off their traditional hunting grounds, farther and farther into the forests. Soon terrible things were happening in Tasmania. Aborigines were killed. Sometimes the they were hunted just for fun, on foot or on horseback, or they were made to work as slaves on the farm or in the houses of the white settlers. The Aborigines began to fight back. They attacked the colonists, burned farms and killed farm animals.

A terrible place

In 1830 the government decided to move the Aborigines to another island, Flinders Island, 40 km off the coast of Tasmania. The soldiers hunted them out of the forests and put them on ships to Flinders Island. There, slowly, far away and out of sight, they died. They had no forests to hunt in. They was nothing for them to do. It was colder and windier there. They got ill and many died. By 1855 there were only sixteen Tasmanian Aborigines still alive.

A population disappears

At last the British moved them back to their island, but things didn't improve. In 1876 the last Tasmanian Aborigine died and that was the end of a whole population. Her name was Truganini. Eventually her body was dug up and her skeleton, strung on wires and upright in a box, was for many years the most popular exhibit in the Tasmanian Museum.

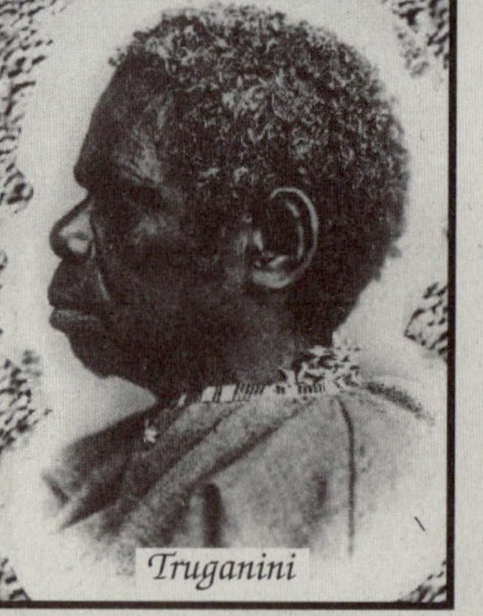

Truganini

Adapted from:
Heaven's Command by James Morris

b *Think of suitable sub-headings for the different parts of the story. Write them in the boxes in the text.*

c *Read the text again quickly and mark one sentence that gives the main point of the whole story.*

d *Go through the text and underline words you don't know.*
- *Mark in blue words that aren't really important for the general understanding of the text.*
- *Mark in red words that you need to understand.*
- *Tick the words in red that you can guess from the context. Look up the words you can't guess.*

e *Make notes on the text on a mind map. Look at page 42 of this workbook for some ideas.*

p. 59/3

5 ▶ The Aboriginal Flag

Translate this text in your exercise book.

The Aboriginal Flag was designed by Harold Thomas, an artist and an Aborigine, in 1971. He wanted it to be a symbol for the Aborigine people, of their race and identity. The black symbolizes the people, the red the earth and their relationship to the land, and the yellow the sun, the giver of life. The Australian and Aborigine athlete Cathy Freeman held the flag, together with the official Australian flag, when she won her gold medal at the Olympic Games in Sydney. The official Australian flag includes the British Union Flag, and many Australians, including many Aborigines, don't feel comfortable with this. But when asked if the Aboriginal flag could be the new Australian flag, Harold Thomas did not agree.

▶▶▶ Now you

Should the Australians change their flag? If so, what flag should they choose? Give your opinion.

I think the Australians should have their own special flag and not one that includes the British flag. But I don't think they should take the Aboriginal flag because the Australian population is made up of people from so many places and it wouldn't be fair to pick out just one group.

p. 59/3

6 ▶ I'm used to her being around

Join the sentences. Use a gerund with its own subject.

1 My sister is always around. I'm used to it. *I'm used to my sister being around.*

2 She's going to university soon. I'm not looking forward to it.

I'm not looking forward to her going to university.

3 We sometimes get into trouble with our parents. She's often responsible.

She's often responsible for us getting into trouble with our parents.

4 I sometimes go out with her friends. Mum and Dad don't like it.

Mum and Dad don't like me going out with her friends.

5 She borrows my CDs. I don't mind that.

I don't mind her borrowing my CDs.

6 She lends them to her friends. I don't like that.

I don't like her lending them to her friends.

7 She's leaving home soon. I hate the idea of it.

I hate the idea of her leaving home.

p59/3

7 Revision Did you know?

Complete the conversation. Use the simple past or the present perfect.

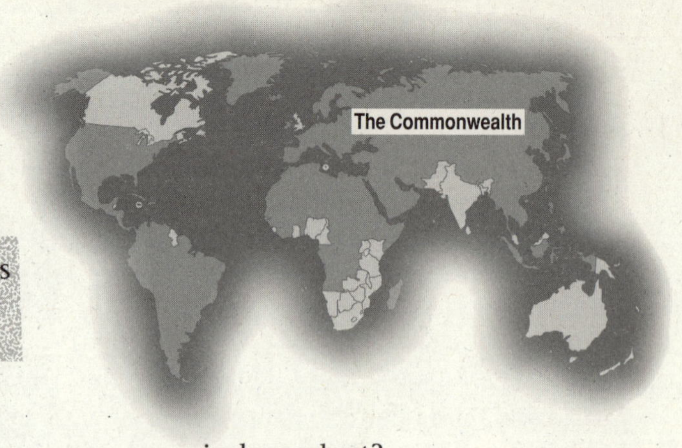

tip Look at p. 138 of the student's book for help on when to use the simple past and present perfect.

LAURA How long (India/be) *has India been* ______ independent?

INDIRA Since 1947.

LAURA And how long (it/be) *was it* ______ a colony of Britain?

INDIRA Er, from 1858, so it (be) *was* ______ a colony for nearly a hundred years.

LAURA And is it a member of the Commonwealth?

INDIRA Yes, it (be) *has been* ______ a member since independence.

LAURA I think some countries (become) *became* ______ independent much earlier.

INDIRA That's true. Australia for example (be) *has been* ______ independent since 1901. But Jamaica (not become) *didn't become* ______ independent until 1962.

LAURA What about the USA? I read that it (be) *was* ______ a colony of Britain too.

INDIRA Yes, but the USA (be) *has been* ______ independent since 1783. The Americans (get) *got* ______ their independence over two hundred years ago.

LAURA A lot of colonies (join) *joined* ______ the Commonwealth when they (leave) *left* ______ the Empire. And some even (keep) *kept* ______ the British queen.

INDIRA True, but Ireland (not join) *didn't join* ______ . And the USA isn't a member either.

8 ▶ Simple or progressive?

Do you need the simple form or the progressive form in these sentences? Underline the forms which are possible here.

1 Who [does this coat belong to? / is this coat belonging to?] It [smells / is smelling] of smoke.

2 You [always borrow / 're always borrowing] my ruler. You [need / 're needing] to buy one of your own.

3 Oh dear. That dog [looks / is looking] at me very aggressively.
– I know what you [mean. / are meaning.] He [looks / is looking] very unfriendly.

4 We [have / 're having] a party next week. Everybody [comes. / is coming.]
– [Does John come? / Is John coming?] – Of course. He [always comes. / 's always coming.]

p.62/5

9 **Revision** But you said …

This person was happier before her holiday. Complete her letter to the travel agent. Use indirect speech.

1 Is the apartment near the sea?

2 Are there beds for four adults?

3 Are dogs allowed ?

4 I want to go somewhere quiet.

5 Is the weather good in May?

6 Please check the dates on the tickets.

Oh yes, madam, of course madam.

I'm writing to tell you that I was very disappointed with the holiday that I booked with your firm. We had a number of problems and I list them below:

1 I asked you before I booked *if the apartment was near the sea*.
In fact we had to walk 5 km to the nearest beach.

2 I asked *if there were beds for four adults*.
I had to sleep on the sofa all week.

3 I asked you *if dogs are/were allowed*.
The first thing I saw when I arrived was a sign saying 'No dogs'.

4 I asked *if the weather is good in May*.
It rained every day.

5 I said *that I wanted to go somewhere quiet*.
Our flat was between a disco and a bar.

6 I asked *you to check the date on the tickets*.
But you put the wrong date on, so we had to leave two days earlier than we wanted to.

10 ▶ **Get the right message**

It's not always easy to understand someone with a strong accent. What would you say if you didn't understand the underlined words?

tip Try and be as specific as you can. Don't say 'Can you repeat that?' every time!

1 Hi. I'm <u>Terence Goolagong</u>. *I'm afraid I didn't get your name. Could you say it again please?*

2 You can phone me at <u>00 72 2467239</u>. *Sorry, what number did you say, please?*

3 I live in <u>Goondiwindi</u> in Queensland. *Sorry, where did you say you live, please?*

4 That's <u>seventeen ninety-five</u> please. *Sorry, how much did you say?*

5 Today there's Kangaroo Stew, Ayers Rock Pie, Crocodile Soup, Outback Pizza … *What kind of pie was that, please?*

p.62/7

Unit 5 Now you can ...

11 ▶ ... talk to a net pal

An Australian girl (Pwrgirl) is on an exchange in Britain. She is chatting in a chatroom with an Australian net pal (Megaboy) about her trip. Write Megaboy's questions.

London Chat

London Capital Chat

Connected persons:
Megaboy
Nina(w) CV Write.
New1(m) CV Write.
Pwrgirl CV Write.

Megaboy: (When – arrive – London?) *When did you arrive in London* ?

Pwrgirl: 4 days ago.

Megaboy: (see – cricket match – yet?) *Have you seen a cricket match yet?*

Pwrgirl: No, not yet! I spent the first 2 days sleeping.

Megaboy: (still – feel tired – after – trip?) *Are you still feeling / Do you still feel tired after the trip?*

Pwrgirl: No, I'm OK now.

Megaboy: (Who – stay with?) *Who are you staying with?*

Pwrgirl: An English family.

Megaboy: (like – them?) *Do you like them?*

Pwrgirl: They are all really nice. They're always asking me if I'm OK.

Megaboy: (rain – all the time – since – you arrive?) *Has it been raining// Has it rained all the time since you arrived?*

Pwrgirl: Of course it hasn't. It doesn't rain all the time, you know!

Megaboy: (people – always talk about – weather ?) *Are people always talking about the weather?*

Pwrgirl: Of course they're not! I think you have a lot of prejudices about the Brits! But yesterday I did hear two people commenting on the weather. Happy???

12 ▶ ... say it a different way

Complete these sentences without using the word 'very'.

tip If you get stuck, look at the blue box at the bottom of page 160 for help.

1 I think it's *completely* normal to feel this way. I'm sure you're *deeply* disappointed.

2 It was *totally* wrong of me to do that and I'm *terribly* sorry.

3 I'm *really* happy to hear your news. I'm sure you'll be *highly* successful in the future.

4 I'm *fully* aware of the difficult situation and I was *greatly* impressed by your performance.

13 ▶ ... get advice about a foreign country

How do you say these things in English?

1 Welche Kleidung eignet sich für eine Wanderung im Busch?

What clothes are suitable for walking in the bush?

2 Dauert es lange, bevor man sich an ein tropisches Klima gewöhnt?

Does it take long to get used to a tropical climate?

3 Was ist die Entfernung zwischen Australien und Indonesien?

What distance is it between Australia and Indonesia?

4 Man sollte sich der Gefahren bewusst sein.

You should be aware of the dangers.

5 Ich habe nichts dagegen, wenn die Verhältnisse schwierig sind.

I don't mind if conditions are tough.

6 Wenn ich pleite bin, könnte ich vielleicht eine Teilzeitbeschäftigung bekommen und Geld verdienen.

If I'm broke, perhaps I could get a part-time job and earn some money.

14 ▶ ... write a story

Prepare to write a story in your exercise book about an accident that happened to you. It could be a serious accident or a silly accident, it doesn't matter. Before you start make some notes.

a *Complete the table below.*

WHO	
WHAT	
WHERE	
WHEN	
HOW	
WHY	

b *Other things to think about:*
- *How did you feel at different times in the story?* (e.g. puzzled, weak, worried, scared ...)
- *Think of an interesting start for your story.*
- *Will you use direct or indirect speech?*

c *Now write your story. Don't forget to use time expressions* (e.g. suddenly, at first, after that, for a moment/second ...) *and linking words* (e.g. although, because, so).

From Mindmapping to Writing a Text

1 ▶ Getting an overview of a grammar rule

a *Look at this mind map. Write a few sentences to explain when you use* 'some' *and* 'any' *in English.*

____

____

____

b *Complete the mind map on the* simple past. *Use the words in the box as labels, but add your own ideas and examples, too.*

be • didn't • irregular • main verb NEGATIVE STATEMENT • QUESTION

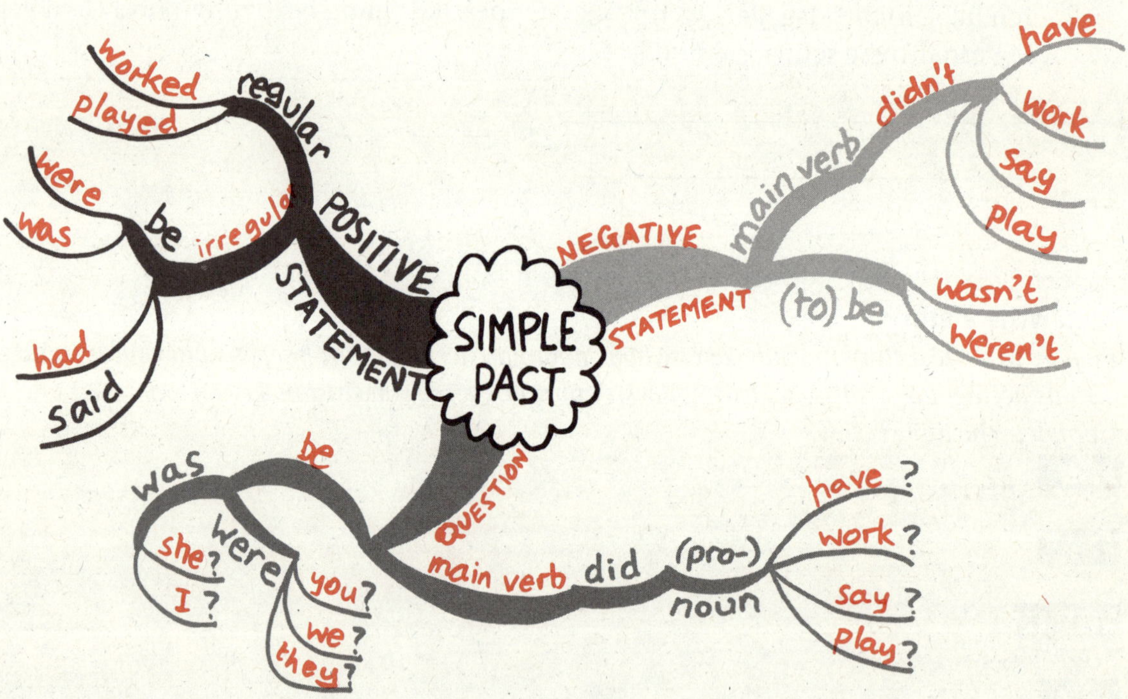

2 ▶ To make notes for a presentation

In your exercise book make a mind map for a short talk on either 'Future plans' or 'Planning a trip to Australia'.

p. 86

3 ▶ **Helping you understand a text**

Read the text and complete the mind map in your exercise book.

Helping the Brits understand the Germans

Why is it that the Brits and the Germans sometimes don't agree? Ben Barkow and Stefan Zeidenitz think the British need to work harder at understanding the Germans and have written a rather funny book to help them. Here are some of the important points:

- The Germans call it 'Ordnung', we can translate it as 'orderliness'. This is definitely important for them and the British find this rather boring. But Barkow says that we should realise that for the Germans life is made up of two halves – public and private – and in private the Germans are very different.
- The Germans find our way of discussing the weather all the time very silly. We find their way of discussing 'serious' things all the time a bit heavy. If you ask a German 'How are you?' they will tell you in great detail. If you don't want to know, don't ask!
- The Germans take their humour very seriously. They like British humour, but German jokes don't translate well.
- The Germans are great hand-shakers: you must shake hands on meeting, parting, arriving, and on agreeing or even on agreeing to disagree.

Adapted from: *Daily Mail*

4 ▶ **Writing a text**

a *Add your own ideas about 'Germans' to the mind map you have already started, or maybe use some of these ideas:* health, 'Sie' and 'du', music, the environment, cars, animals, 'Gemütlichkeit'.

b *Write a few sentences using the mind map. The box on the right has words that might help you to link your ideas.*

In my opinion • To give an example • For example
Firstly • Secondly • That's why • Why not have ...?
Finally, I'd like to say that ... • To sum up

⚠ *These suggested answers are also adapted from* Xenophobe's Guide to the Germans *by Stefan Zeidenitz and Ben Barkow, Ravette Publishing, 1993:*

- *The Germans are very interested in their health and their bathrooms are full of medicine and pills. One German illness doesn't exist in Britain: Kreislaufstörung.*
- *You call people 'Sie' until you know them well, then you call them 'du'. The older person or the woman offers the 'du' to the younger person or the man.*
- *Germans love their cars more than they love children. If your car is really expensive, you must be really important. Germans also love dogs more than children.*
- *Wessies say that Ossies are lazy and complain all the time. Ossies say Wessies are arrogant and only care about themselves.*

p. 87

Paraphrasing

tip Look again at page 88 of your student's book for help with paraphrasing.

1 ▶ What do they mean?

You almost certainly don't know some of these words. But can you guess what the person means?

1 The bus stop is next to the graveyard. Oh, you don't know what graveyard means? Well, it's a place, sometimes near a church, where they put dead people.

'Graveyard' in German is probably: *Friedhof*

2 The hotel is very near junction 15. A junction? It's the place where there are roads that go onto and come off the motorway. If you look on the map, you can see they have numbers. There's junction 15.

'Junction' is probably: *Ab- oder Ausfahrt*

3 Do you like package holidays? They are holidays where everything is organised for you, the place that you stay, the flight, all in one package.

'Package holiday' is probably: *Pauschalreise*

2 ▶ Explain these words

a *Complete the dialogues between Ann and Uli.*

ULI She's wearing a great *Parfum*.
ANN What's she wearing? That's a German word.
ULI I thought it was the same word in English. It's *stuff you put on when you go out. It smells nice*.
ANN Oh, you mean '<u>per</u>fume'.

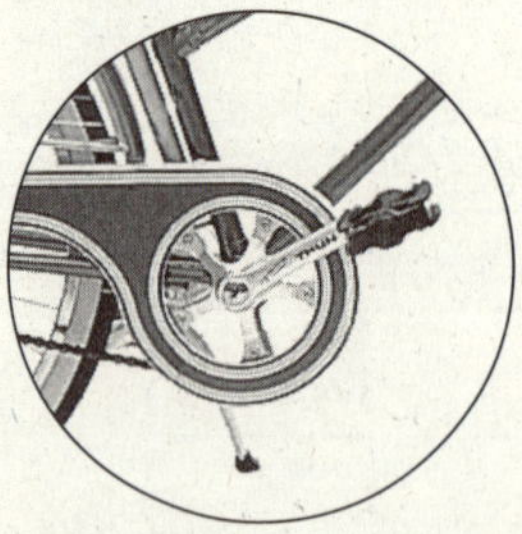

ULI There's a problem with the er ...
ANN Eh? Where's the problem?
ULI *They're the part of a bike that you put your feet on.*
ANN Oh you mean the pedals!

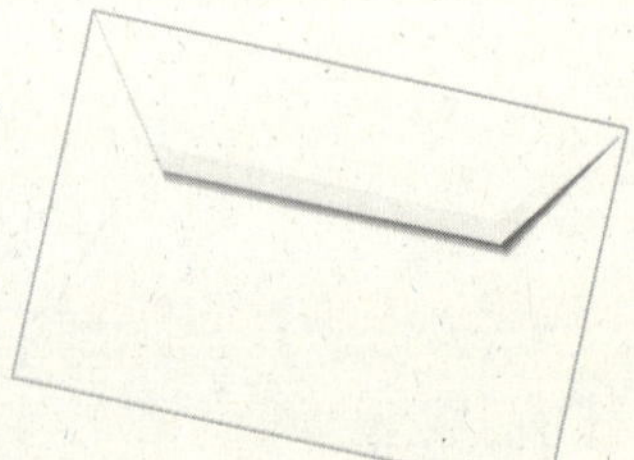

ULI Have you got a ... Er, well I've written a letter to my parents ...
ANN Do you need a stamp?
ULI No, I need a ... *it's the thing that you put a letter into*.
ANN Oh, you mean an envelope.

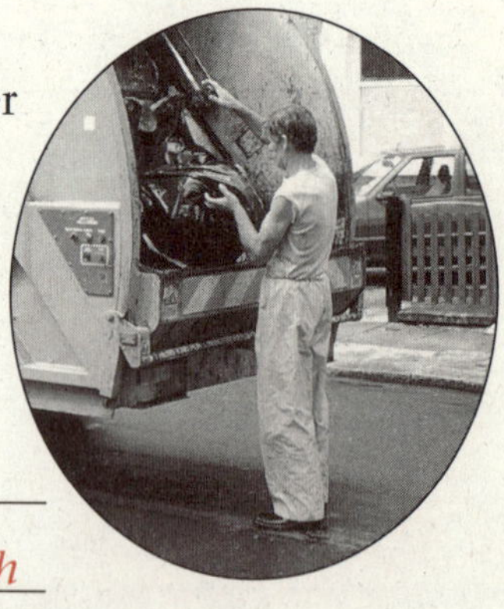

ULI I just saw the er ... there are two men outside.
ANN Who?
ULI You know, ... *the men that take the rubbish* .
ANN Oh the dustmen! Oh good. Quick: let's put the rubbish out!

b *Paraphrase these German words in English. Write the descriptions in your exercise book.*

1 Zahnspange
2 Hagel
3 Geisterfahrer
4 Scheibenwischer
5 Hecke
6 Heuschnupfen

p. 88

How to Use a Grammar

1 ▶ Find it in your grammar book

Where would you find help with these problems in the grammar book that you usually use? Note down the numbers of useful pages and answer the questions if you can.

tip You need a grammar book to do these exercises! It doesn't matter which one it is.

Page in your grammar book		Question	Answer
141	1	In German I can use an adjective as a noun. So instead of *die reichen Leute*, I can say *die Reichen*. Can you do that in English?	*Yes, but only with plurals.*
148	2	I'm bad at word order. I don't know where to put words like *always, sometimes, often* and *never* in a sentence. Is there a simple rule?	*There are three main rules, but they are not very simple.*
195	3	Someone told me that you can use *that* for people and for things in relative clauses. Is that true?	*Yes, in spoken English.*
108	4	Can you use a participle after *to see*, as in *I saw him running*? Or does it have to be *I saw him run*?	*It can be both.*
146	5	Adverbs go with verbs, right? So I should say *Emmeline looks prettily*, but that's wrong, isn't it?	*That's wrong. It should be 'She looks pretty'.*
16	6	I want to say *Du kommst, nicht wahr?* in English. The first bit is OK: *You're coming, …?* But what do I say for *nicht wahr*?	*'… aren't you?'*
23 f	7	We're doing 'the passive with modal auxiliaries'. I've got two questions: a) What are *modal auxiliaries*?	*Words like 'can', 'must', 'may'.*
77		b) How do you make a passive with them?	*M.A. + 'be' + past participle*
109	8	How do you say *machen lassen* in English? You don't use *let*, do you? So what do you use?	*You use 'have' + object + past participle.*

2 ▶ Using a grammar to explain mistakes

Imagine you are helping a friend in Year 7 with his/her English. Your student has made a lot of mistakes in a test. In your exercise book, make notes on:
a) what the correct form would be and b) what the rule is.

article	(The) life in Britain changed when the Romans invaded. They ruled Britannia from
gerund	43 AD until 410 AD and loved (build.) They built good straight roads with forts
pron modal	and towns along (they.) So their soldiers (can moved) about the countryside
adverb	(quick) when there was any trouble (and there was!). The Romans also built

p. 91

How to Write a Summary

tip Look at pages 98/99 of your student's book if you need help.

1 ▶ What is important?

Can you remember what you have learned about summaries?
In your exercise book, write down the main points under these headings:
– the choice of information from the text
– the structure of a summary
– the form and style of a summary

2 ▶ The fight for the Amazon

The following report by Sting tells you about his journey into the heart of Brazil as part of his campaign to save the jungle[1].

a *Read through the text carefully twice and make notes on the most important details. Tip: It might help to ask yourself the 'wh-questions'.*

b *Write your summary in your exercise book, aiming at 600–800 words (the report on these pages is 1200 words long). When you've finished, check it for style, fluency and correctness.*

In February 1989 I return to Brazil. With me is Jean-Pierre Dutilleux, a French film crew and Red Crow, Chief of the Dakota Sioux. We have two aims. We hope to persuade President Sarney to agree to our plans for a Rainforest Foundation[2]; and we need a passport for Raoni (chieftain[3] of the Indian tribes of the lower Xingu river) to join our tour of the developed countries to collect money for the Foundation.

It is over a year since my last visit, when I sat in a jungle clearing[4] with Raoni as he drew a map of the Xingu in the sand. He pointed to three Indian reservations and spoke of his own dream to join these reservations with the huge unexplored area of the National Park.

'I need money to set up the park with clear borders and I need the world to know about it so that it can survive. Every year the burning of the forest by the white man gets closer and closer. You must help me stop it or there'll be no forest left.'

Fernando Mesquita, minister and friend of the Brazilian President is at home. We describe our plan of a Xingu National Park with money from Europe, North America and Japan. We tell him we would like to work as partners with the Brazilian government. Can he help us? Can he arrange a meeting with the President? He gets up. 'I will call the President.'

After three minutes the minister returns, smiling. 'He will meet you at 11.30 in the morning at the palace.' So far, so good.

The President, a good-looking man with grey hair, is waiting for us and welcomes us into his library. After 45 minutes of discussion and looking at maps, the President agrees that, in general, he will support our project. He has given us the green light.

It's getting late and we must arrive in the jungle before it gets dark. There are no landing lights, no computers. The pilot has only his eyes – and so we need daylight.

The land below us is greener than it was during my last journey. It's the end of the rainy season and in a few months there will be only red dust.

After two hours the beauty of the jungle is below us, wild and mysterious. Then, suddenly, all the trees are gone, cut down. We see a few cows in clearings as big as Central Park.

The plane lands and Raoni is waiting for us with about a hundred Indians. I am very excited to be back here. Raoni welcomes us all warmly. We tell him about the meeting with the President and lay the map out for the elders[5]. As night comes, they all look very happy. The Indians cook us a dinner of fish and rice. I'm too excited to sleep. Up at sunrise to wash in the river. Every square centimetre of the forest is alive.

Soon we leave again and fly over jungle where some of the Indians have never seen a white person. We will spend the night with the Kayapo in a village on the edge of the unexplored forest.

It's strange to see Raoni in our plane, proud in his chieftain's head-dress and body paint, in the middle of our technology. The first time he saw his forest from a plane must have been wonderful for him, but with this gift comes a danger: we can see huge areas of destruction. There are farms already inside the borders of the park we want. Raoni is upset by how near and how big they are.

The village we are going to has had very little contact with the outside world. We are flying over another planet – a dream of silver and green. It is amazing to see an Indian village from the air: it's like travelling to another century. We land and turn off the engines. All around us there is silence – and then we see the Indians watching us.

The tribe look frightening, their bodies painted black. The men have wooden plates in their mouths. The women have the tops of their heads shaved[6], and black face make-up. It is the meeting of two alien[7] cultures.

The chief arrives to welcome us, an old man with a head-dress of white eagle feathers[8]. We get out the map and explain about the park. The Indians have a way of looking at you which kind of opens you up. It would be hard to lie to these people.

The next day we make our way to Raoni's village by boat down the Xingu. I've been looking forward to the river trip since we got here. I sit under a bright red umbrella.

We travel with the flow of the river. The great rivers of Europe and North America must have looked like this centuries ago. Once again, I feel like a time traveller. As the sun begins to sink, the sky changes to fire and everyone is quiet as our shadows run like dark gods across the water.

In the last moments before the sun sinks, we see something move in the water on the opposite bank. As we get closer we see that all the children and young people of the village are in the river.

This welcome is so beautiful, it is hard not to cry.

A storm has now begun and the rain begins to fall. Too tired to eat, we fall asleep.

The next morning we go to check the runway[9], hoping that the heavy rain hasn't damaged it too badly. The children follow us. There's lots of mud. It doesn't look too good, and we need to be back in Brasilia today.

As the morning mist disappears we sit on our bags, waiting. Our planes circle the runway. They try several times to land and, at last, it works. Then we take off and wave goodbye to Raoni's village.

As we fly south we see huge dark clouds in front of us. There is no way around them. Our small plane flies into the great wall of cloud. We can't see a thing and the noise of the rain on the windows is terribly loud. We seem to be flying underwater.

We are thrown around like a child's toy. I realize that the rainforest could destroy us at any moment. Our brave little plane struggles[10] on. The pilot is nervously fighting to control the plane. We must be out of this soon.

At last the sun comes through the clouds, we see the forest below and the pilot relaxes. Everything is quiet. And then comes the news on the radio that our second plane has crash-landed[11]. After what we have just been through, the shock is too much. The radio is difficult to understand but at last it becomes clear that our friends are safe.

Well, our trip has been successful: We've made many friends and got into the newspapers. We have Raoni's passport, the government is behind us, and, maybe the most important thing, I think the people of Brazil are too. Now it's up to the world.[12] That night I fly north back to London. Below me in the darkness is the Amazon rainforest.

I will be back.

Adapted from: *Jungle Stories* by Sting

[1] jungle ['dʒʌŋgl] *Dschungel* [2] foundation [faʊn'deɪʃn] *Stiftung*
[3] chieftain ['tʃi:ftən] *Stammesführer* [4] clearing ['klɪərɪŋ] *Lichtung*
[5] elders ['eldəz] *(Stammes-)Älteste* [6] shave [ʃeɪv] *rasieren*
[7] alien ['eɪliən] *fremd* [8] eagle feather ['i:gl 'feðə] *Adlerfeder*
[9] runway *Start-/Landebahn* [10] struggle ['strʌgl] *kämpfen*
[11] crash-land [ˌ-'-] *bruchlanden*
[12] Now it's up to the world. *Jetzt liegt es an der Welt.*

p. 98/99

18

SKILLS OPTION

Writing Letters

Imagine you are planning a trip to Britain and want to write to the British Tourist Authority for some information.

a *Think about these points:*

- Where do you want to go? (London, the coast, the Scottish Highlands, ...)
- Who are you going with? (Your family, a youth group, your class next year, ...)
- Where do you want to stay? (Camp-site, hotel, ...)
- Do you want advice on special interests? (Language courses, horse riding, ...)

b *Complete the letter below, perhaps using phrases from the formal letter on page 100 of your student's book. It might be a good idea to plan your letter on a mind map before you start.*

tip Look at page 100 in your student's book and note down in your exercise book five things it tells you about writing a formal letter.

Karl-Kunger-Str. 6
12435 Berlin
Germany

28 March 2004

British Tourist Authority
Black's Road
London W6 9EL
England

Dear *Sir or Madam*

I am visiting Britain *this summer with a group of students from my school. We would like to visit the north-west of Scotland because we have heard that it is very beautiful.*
We would be very grateful for any information you can send us about where we could stay.
We would prefer a camp-site to a hotel.
Some of us have special interests: if you could recommend places to climb mountains and go swimming, it would be very helpful.
Thank you in advance for your help.

I look *forward to hearing from you in the near future.*

Yours faithfully

Lisa Raue

p. 100